Homeschooling 101 Philosophy for Kids and Teenagers

Historical Philosophy as a Way of Life & Parental Guidance for Youth to Embrace Social Skills, Logical Thinking to Become Intelligent Adults

Loria Lacerda

Table of Contents

Metaphysics
What is Reality
Are Things We can't Touch Real?
Is this World Real or am I Dreaming?
Is time Real or an Illusion?
Which is the Person, the Body or the Mind?
What is the Meaning of Life?
What is Free will?
Is God Real?
If God is Real, Why do Bad Things Happen?
What is a Soul?
Do Animals Have Souls?
Why are people scared to Die?
When I die, where do I go?

Ethics
What is good? and what is bad?
What is the difference between good and bad?
Do Animals have a Concept of good and bad?
How do Our Actions Affect Other People?
If I punch Someone because He punched Me first, does it make Me a bad Person
Is it disrespectful if I disagree with My Parents or Teachers?
If I do bad things with good intentions, does that make me a Bad person?
What is Conscience?
What Are My Obligations to My Parents?
What are My Parents' Obligations to Me?
How can I be happy?
How do I know it's Love?

Epistemology
What is the Truth?
What is Knowledge?
What is the Difference between Knowledge and Belief?
What is Skepticism?

Logic
Could Time Travel be possible?
Could the Multiverse be Real?
Why Do People Dream?
If Someone makes a clone of you, are you still you?

Aesthetics
What is Beauty?
Could One thing be Beautiful and ugly at the same time?
What is Art?

Axiology
What has Value?
Is Money Really Valuable

Political Philosophy
What is Freedom?

What is the difference between Justice and Revenge?
What would happen if the Law is the same for all?

Conclusion

Introduction

Philosophy sounds pretty serious and complicated, right? To adults maybe, yes. But to someone younger, philosophy could simply be vague statements elaborated using deeper meanings.

Is philosophy for adults only? Aren't children capable of being philosophers at a young age? Of course not! It's actually better to start harnessing that inner philosopher as early as possible.

Young people have a very keen interest on the world around them. But it needs to be consistently tapped and exercised. Children are undoubtedly, ***"natural philosophers"***, with a strong pull towards wonders and fascinations. Children are keen observers and are very curious of the things they have no idea about. Looking for the answers to questions is the most important characteristic of a philosopher, one that comes natural of children.

If you take a closer look, some children are actually better philosophers than adults, because children are always curious of the things they still don't know, while some adults, not all, acts as if they know everything, which is far from possible.

Philosophy is a guiding principle. It could be in expressed in many forms such as a motto, sayings, proverbs, quotations, personal convictions, point of view, or an outlook in life. Actually, children have been living with philosophy; but just might not realize that those are already philosophical ideas. The famous quotations we know are actually line of famous philosophers in history, stated out of answering philosophical questions which arose during their time.

Are you familiar with the following quotes?

"Time is gold."

"It's better late than never."

"Birds of the same feather flock together."

"Cleanliness is next to godliness."

"Practice makes perfect."

It's pretty cliché to read these quotations but they are actually examples of philosophies which have guided us in our everyday life.

Philosophy isn't like a license that we only need to get when you're of legal age. Philosophy is not something we learn overnight or something that can only be of use in isolated situations.

Unlike popular belief, philosophy is actually part of our daily life. To master it and utilize it effectively, you need to start early. It's not that hard to understand. You might even be surprised how interesting it is and how often you think, talk, and act like the famous philosophers in history, without even knowing it.

In chapter 1, you will understand more about philosophy by tracing its roots, knowing its features and the factors that might affect one's philosophy.

Children as Natural Philosophers

Children can be compared to clay because their true forms are yet to be molded. But although they are influenced both by internal and external factors, they are philosophers by nature, and sometimes, asked greater number of questions every day.

They have a lot of things to know and even the simplest things easily ignite their attention and curiosity. Children are generally very insightful and intuitive. Even if they have more to explore about the world, they can already see connections between things and ideas, and would often start philosophical question-and-answer portions with their parents and other adults. These questions should not be overlooked rather should be answered appropriately to develop their innate philosopher even more.

Yes, they have less knowledge of the proper terminologies and explanations, and still lack the cognitive capabilities to do so, they have what is essential to being a philosopher – they have a wide imagination, and imagination is the key to intuition.

Adults bombard them with children stories, fairytales, online videos, bedtime stories, legends, and myths. These may serve as past times, or things that can make them pre-occupied while mum and dad are busy with other stuff, but these materials unconsciously help build up their imagination. Sooner or later they begin creating their own stories and scripts while playing Barbie or Spiderman toys.

Their imagination is limitless. Children stitch up their understanding of the world through it, seeing it from a different, creative perspective. They have both imagination and intuition and are quite excellent with it. When you present them with questions, they are willing to answer as much as they could, as much as they are excited to know whether they are right or wrong, and when they're wrong, they are willing to learn the right answers to your questions.

We can say that when it comes to arguments, children are also fearless. They are generally very honest. They let their ideas flow without fear of being right or wrong.

Chapter 1 - Understanding Philosophy

What is Philosophy?

The word, philosophy, comes from the Greek words, ***"philia"*** which means "love", and ***"sophia"*** which means "wisdom". Therefore, philosophy literally means ***"a love of wisdom"***, a desire to know more and develop a questioning nature, and a sense of wonder.

It originated in Greece, wherein a lot of schools of thought emerged. In philosophy, a school of thought is not a place where we take classes with other kids. It means a ***"way of thinking"***, or ideas about a topic, shared by many others. Philosophy is the development of your ideas.

What we know of this world will always be partial, because there are limitless questions that need answering. Knowledge and understanding is always incomplete. Philosophy is the deeper search for meaning and understanding about ourselves, our existence, our surroundings, our world, and the universe itself.

Philosophy teaches you not only what to think of, but how to think. Moreover, it teaches to raise questions, entertain those questions, and search for the answers. It clarifies that questioning is not an insult, but a form of discovery, and questioning is the foundation of everything that has been discovered, invented, and established in our world.

Alexander Graham Bell couldn't have invented the telephone if he didn't ask himself the question "Is it possible to talk to a friend if they're far away?"

Wilbur and Orville Wright couldn't have built the world's first successful motor-operated airplane, if they didn't ask "Can people fly like birds in the sky?"

It all starts with a question. The essence of philosophy is to encourage questions, in order to form new concepts and ideas. In simple terms, philosophy makes you ask not just questions, but good ones. "Why?", "Why do I have to?", "How?", "What if?", and the likes.

As early as toddler age, we begin to unlock our inner philosopher.

For Example: *When we were little, we were taught that the pet at home is called a "dog".*

Now, we knew little of what a dog is and we conceptualized a dog as furry, four-legged, barks, and wags its tail.

But later on, we were corrected by our parents when we called a cat, a dog as well. This is when we start refining our ideas.

We started asking questions "If not all with fur and four legs are called dogs, what's makes a dog?"

We begin knowing more about dogs, and as we grew up, even learned of the different breeds of dogs, and how to take care of each of them.

As we continue questioning ourselves and the world, our philosophy widens. Moreover, we learn to defend them or change them if someone else disproves them. Philosophy is important because it serves as our basis for judgment in making choices and decisions.

Elements of Philosophy

Philosophy begins with a question which makes you want to get down to the bottom of things.

- **Articulation**
    - Stating your ideas clearly, in words that can easily be understood by other people

For Example: *Admit it or not, you also have that "favorite" teacher that you prefer listening to over another teacher, even of the same subject or discipline.*

This is because your favorite teacher is more "articulate" and explains lessons and instructions more understandable than other teachers you encounter every day. Let's say, you excel in their subject because they explain really well. They are articulate.

- **Argument**
    - Justifying your ideas, opinions, and principles, in contrast with that of other people, to prove yourself correct, and establish a conclusion
    - Look at the examples below. Tell me if it stirs up a debate inside you. An argument makes you want to justify your answer upon agreeing or disagreeing with it.

  For Example: *If you offend a kid at school, you offend their parents too.*

  Education depends on the school you go to. Schools in the city deliver better education than those in the provinces.

- **Analysis**
    - Analyzing your ideas by determining and understanding the details or breaking down a certain concept into several parts to be understood

  For Example: *In one of your classes, you encountered an unfamiliar word, and found it difficult to follow in the discussion.*

  To analyze is to break down the word into parts. An unfamiliar word would have to undergo a very quick structural analysis, where you try to look for context clues or word affixes, and decode the meaning of the word.

- **Synthesis**

- Tailoring together all the pieces of ideas you have into a single, unified idea.
- Combining one or more ideas to come up with a more updated and complete view.

For Example: *One easy example of synthesis is coming up with your own definition or explanation of a difficult science terminology or topic.*

Let's say the teacher gives a seatwork wherein you are to explain "philosophy" in your own words, including as much information as you could. Synthesis is remembering all the ideas in your head that is related to philosophy; stitch it together, in order to finish the seatwork.

Brief History of Philosophy

Philosophy began in the Greek city-state of "Miletus", the wealthiest city, reestablished during the Ionian period. This is where the first known western philosopher, "Thales", originated and was later known as "Thales of Miletus".

It is in this city that he asked the first philosophical questions.

"Is there something (reality) that does not change in a world where everything is constantly changing?"

"If yes, what is this reality and is there only one reality or does it have many forms?"

"What is the basic element of the universe from which everything else comes from?"

Thales of Miletus challenged the long-running traditions of Greece and argued that the world is not controlled by gods, goddesses, and mythology, but by natural causes, which awaited to be explored and studied. The first philosophy of the earth is from Thales of Miletus who believed that the Earth floats in water.

Aside from Thales, one of the first philosophers was his pupil, Anaximander, who was the first to have his ideas written down, since nothing was written by Thales. But unlike his mentor, Anaximander did not believe that water is the first cause of how the Earth came to be, because water is just another element of Earth. Rather he believed the first cause was beyond water, is infinite, and boundless. He called his first cause, *"apeiron"*.

Timeline of Philosophy

- **Mythological Period (1800 B.C. – 300 B.C.)**
  Period wherein legends and mythology, and the belief in gods and goddesses explain natural phenomena

- **Pre-Socratic/Natural Philosophy (600 B.C. – 370 B.C.)**
  Opposed mythological beliefs and introduced critical thinking and reasoning to explain natural phenomena

- **Period of Philosophy's Big Three (430 B.C. – 322 B.C.)**
  The most important names in philosophy came to be – Socrates, Plato, and Aristotle

- **Hellenistic Period (323 B.C. – 420 A.D.)**
  Period of Greece's cultural decline and the adaptation of cultures and beliefs from other lands

- **Medieval Period (400 A.D. – 1400 A.D.)**
  Period of Christian theology in relation to the branches of philosophy

- **Renaissance Period (1400 A.D. – 1600 A.D.)**
  Period of the rebirth of culture, religion and politics, after its decline during the Hellenistic period

- **The Scientific Revolution (1543 – 1727)**
  Period of vast scientific discoveries and inventions and the rise of empiricism over rationalism

- **Baroque Period (1600 – 1725)**
    The development of arts and aesthetics was progressive

- **The Enlightenment Period (1650 – 1789)**
    Age of the Transformation, wherein the teaching of the Catholic Church was questioned and philosophy or religion was rampant

- **Romanticism Period (1770 – 1848)**
- **The Modern Day (1850 – 1970)**
- **Contemporary Period (1970 – Present)**

Importance of Philosophy

Philosophy plays a vital role in our daily life, more than we know, and more than what we are conscious of. Listed below are the benefits of philosophy to an individual.

- ✓ Philosophy turns us into a critical thinker who analyzes and rationalizes before making a decision and believing anything. Through philosophy, we learn to weigh the validity of ideas before adopting it as our own.

- ✓ Philosophy makes us deep-thinkers who are always curious for answers which leads to a better understanding of the different concepts around us.

- ✓ Being philosophical doesn't mean being a smarty-pants. Philosophy helps us apply reason and justification in our decisions when faced with real-life situations.

- ✓ Philosophy encourages a positive discussion where people are open to other people's ideas to further expand their own. This helps us think together towards a unified goal. A simple brainstorming activity at school could lead to a lot of realizations.

- ✓ Philosophy makes us curious about the unexplored aspects of life and the world. Curiosity is one of the keys to discovering the unknown. Although a lot has been discovered, invented and proven, there is still more to uncover.

- ✓ Philosophy helps us think outside the box because it awakens our inner eyes. We become more creative and innovative.

- ✓ Philosophy draws to answering questions and never stopping until we find the answer we are looking for. This is a healthy trait a person can carry out even at school or in a workplace someday. With philosophy, we seek answers and we become solution-finders, making us complain less.

- ✓ Philosophy can help us know who we truly are and realize our purpose of living, questions which are considered to be one of the hardest to answer.

- ✓ Philosophy can be considered a moral compass, which guides our actions, directing us to what is generally good, stirring away from what is considered generally bad. With this thought, we become conscientious of our deeds, because we consider the feelings of other people and the possible consequences of our actions. Imagine what the world would be if all of us are conscientious.

- ✓ Being a moral compass, philosophy helps improve the quality of human relationships as people would strive to act accordingly, towards a common good. We are guided by an understanding of our differences and set these differences aside to embrace the individuality of the people around us. When we are guided by philosophy, we value our relationships with other people, thus conflicts are avoided, if not, easily resolved.

- ✓ Philosophy builds up love for knowledge and education, which remains to be the stepping stone to achieving our dreams ins life.

- ✓ Philosophy makes us see the beauty in things, no matter how vague it seems. We see in different perspectives with the goal of finding something to admire about things, instead of focusing on the flaws.

✓ Philosophy creates fairness, equality and open-mindedness in our society since people entertain ideas and concepts new to them, to be examined and evaluated first. Equality and fairness are some of the most controversial societal issues in the world then and now which has sparked conflict among races and nations.

Factors Affecting One's Philosophy

Philosophy may not be absolute at all times. It can also change over time. It doesn't matter how long you've been living up to your philosophy. No matter how rooted, it can still be subjected to changes or slight modifications.

- The Nativity of a Person

     Nativity means your place of origin. We have different upbringing because we don't live under the same roof and come from the same family. When it comes to raising their children, Western and Eastern countries have their similarities and differences.

     Your place of origin, your community, and your family plays a major in the philosophy you believe. What has been instilled in you from childhood will not be easily changed unless you are exposed to a new philosophy which would appear more believable than what your nativity has dictated for as long as you remember.

- One's Total Experiences

     We have a popular saying, "Experience is the best teacher". This is really broad and its meaning depends upon the person. One of the strongest influencers of philosophy is experience.

     Everything we have gone through since childhood affects our principles and beliefs growing up. Some may be positive and uplifting, while some may be negative and destructive.

One's personal experience is also one of the reasons why one doesn't agree with the other in some arguments. They differ in opinion because they have had different lives to live. Let's say a child born with a silver spoon, who has been given a very easy life, might not value the idea of "saving up money for the future", as much as another child born of the middle class and has seen the uncertainty of tomorrow.

- Educational Background

    School also plays a vital role in building the right philosophy in us. Education teaches us right conduct, values, responsibilities, as well as academics, and reasoning, delivered by competent teachers and mentors.

    Being children, you look up to your teachers, and some even want to be like them 10 or 15 years from now. Being a role model to you, you tend to imitate them sometimes, and unconsciously, you acquire the advice they give you in class and adopt in your life. You believe in them so your trust that their words shed light and are unquestionably right.

- Social Heritage

    Social heritage is quite similar to the nativity of a person but is focused on the customs, traditions, folkways, and mores, practice by a person's country of origin.

    China is known for "filial piety", a philosophy focusing on tremendous love and respect for the family, especially for the elders.

    The Japanese have well-respected work ethics, which practices courtesy and respect to authority. This is the Japanese bow to one another. The lower their bow, the higher the authority of the person in front of them, or the deeper the respects and gratitude they have.

The Japanese are also famous for their, minimalistic "clutter-free environment", and believes that maintaining cleanliness is everybody's responsibility.

Chapter 2 – Why Should You Learn about Philosophy?

A. Philosophy in Daily Life

As mentioned earlier, philosophy is part of our daily life. It helps make those countless big and small decisions every single day, and help you handle any situation you might possibly find yourself in.

When you apply philosophy, you do not jump into conclusions but instead, you analyze and listen to other people's opinions. This is a good way to avoid getting yourself in a debate or worse, in a fight. Better yet, you learn to defend your ideas and opinions and persuade your family and friends that you have a point, and they will support and agree with your point of view.

When presented with big ideas, you know how to spot good reasoning and bad reasoning, and you end up having better judgement, because you weigh both sides. In this chapter we will be looking at quite a number of quotes by famous philosophers as they will bring you deeper into the world of philosophy!

"Studying philosophy cultivates doubt without helplessness, and confidence without hubris. I've watched kids evolve to be more rational, skeptical, and open-minded, and I've seen them interact in more fair-minded and collaborative ways. As one 10-year-old said, "I've started to actually solve arguments and problems with philosophy. And it works better than violence or anything else."

~ Michelle Sowey

You become curious and gain interest in subjects which sparks your curiosity. Therefore, philosophy makes you ask more questions about your surroundings, and you look for the answers. You do not settle leaving it in the unknown.

Like Queen Elsa of the Disney movie, "Frozen", you race into the unknown. You just got to know the answers!

This is a very good characteristic if you are to succeed as a student, and even as a future professional. Philosophers actually make a good employee and eventually a good boss because a philosopher is inquisitive, creative, flexible, and continues to know more, especially about the things he still doesn't know.

B. Philosophy at Home

If philosophy makes us ask a lot of questions, who do we usually bombard with questions every day? Our parents, of course! You first learn to question and reason at home, in ways that are sometimes even too much to bear.

A five-year-old would ask his mother endlessly very simple questions the whole wakeful hours of the day, that do not make sense or sound a little funny sometimes.

"Where does the sun go when it goes down at dusk?"

"Why does the moon only show up at night?"

"Do cats really have nine lives?"

"Why do dogs circle around in its place several times before getting some sleep?"

"Why do I have to go to school?"

"Why doesn't it snow in other countries?"

All these questions make sense. There is no such thing as a dumb question.

It takes a lot of patience but your parents are listening. Don't be afraid to ask questions. Asking questions at home helps you formulate ideas, and help you practice your arguments and back up those arguments with proof and examples.

There is nothing wrong with asking your parents some questions. Of course, as young people, we need to follow rule sets inside the house and acquire the philosophy our family has lived by generation by generation.

But it is also important that as an individual, you have insights and opinions which you can call your own, a point of view you can be proud of, and a reasoning power that would leave everyone nodding their heads in astonishment.

C. Philosophy at School

The school is one of the best places to learn and exercise philosophy. Philosophy can help you to become more of a critical thinker.

This means you read more and explore more to understand the things you are taught at school. You analyze your lessons and look into it even more closely. You process and evaluate the information before deciding to believe them to be true.

In schools in Ireland, they have what they call, ***"Thinking Time"***, a weekly session, wherein teachers and students sit in a circle, and spend minutes to hours of discussing topics or the day's lessons, through question and answer, about a topic of choice.

This is like a ***"freedom time"***, where kids can ask, explore, express, and develop thinking skills.

Although methods vary depending on the facilitator, normally, a student will be chosen to raise a question and open a discussion. The child sitting next to him or her will be "tipped", and has the choice whether to share something about the topic or simply pass and tip the next person, so on and so forth.

Like Ireland's Thinking Time, this book encourages young people like you to observe, ask relevant questions, recognize the essence of your questions, look for evidences, evaluate those evidences, suggest solutions, and make important decisions.

When you become used to asking smart and relevant questions, you gain more knowledge and understanding compared to others. This could possibly help improve your grades in various subjects in school. So, don't hesitate to raise your hands in class.

According to studies, children who are introduced to philosophy are more likely to perform better at school and get higher test scores in verbal, numerical, and spatial disciplines.

Philosophy also fosters ***"higher-order thinking skills"***, which is what you showcase when you do activities such as summarizing a passage, analyzing a problem, interpreting a poem, or solving a mystery case.

It will be beneficial for children if the school system will encourage arguments in its original sense of valuing someone's claims, and not only focus on determining a "winner" of the argument, like two dogs playing tug of war for a shoe.

Chapter 3 – The Branches of Philosophy

In chapter 2, it was discussed that philosophy started with early Greeks, spearheaded by Thales of Miletus. We also learned that philosophy uses features such as articulation, argument, analysis, and synthesis and that it can be changed over time since there are factors that can affect it.

Chapter 3 will be presenting the branches of philosophy, and the school of thoughts under each branch. Examples are provided to help process the information a lot easier.

A. Metaphysics

Metaphysics comes from the Greek words, ***"meta"*** which means, "beyond", and ***"physikon"*** which means "nature". It is the branch of philosophy that focuses on the nature of reality and the study of existence. It answers the no-to-simple question, "What is?" Metaphysics explains that, how we see reality depends on how we understand and interpret the things of this world, and we decide and act accordingly.

One of the most basic questions in metaphysics is "Is this world real or just an illusion?" It looks like a very simple question but if you try to answer it on your own, you'll be surprised how difficult it actually is. Philosophical questions such as this one would make you wonder and ponder if what you have believed in all these years is true or not.

The word Metaphysics is said to have originated from Aristotle's book entitled, **"Ta Meta Ta Physika"** which translates as "the book which comes after the book about Physics. Makes sense, right?

Metaphysics has three main branches:

- **Cosmology** – the study of the "cosmos" which seeks to understand the origin, structure, and the natural laws that give and maintain its order.

- **Ontology** – also known as **"the science of being 'qua' (being)"**; deals with reality and existence, and the relationship of existing things with one another.

- **Theology** – the study of the idea of having a "God", several gods, or any form of divinity, controlling the matters of the universe.

Before the concept of science was developed, there was a "natural philosophy", which studies the natural phenomena on Earth, the universe. "Natural philosophy", became "science" later on, because, in Latin, the word *"scientia"* means knowledge, a dominant element of natural philosophy.

Unlike cosmology and ontology, natural philosophy can be explained through experimentation, which followed a standard process, we now know as the "scientific method". So, natural philosophy was renamed into science, by the end of the 18th century.

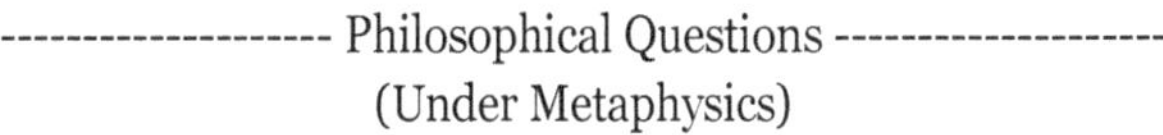

-------------------- Philosophical Questions --------------------
(Under Metaphysics)

1. What is real?

    Have you ever asked yourself upon waking up if the world you live in is real or just another dream? The question, "Is this real?" is not as simple as it seems.

    Can we plainly say that everything that is tangible (can be touched) is real, and everything else that is intangible (cannot be touched) is not real?

    Can we base reality on our senses – that only what we can see, fear, touch, taste, and feel are to be considered as real?

Philosophy argues that "reality" is how we perceive it to be. What we think is real comes from our consciousness of ourselves as a being, living in this world. Therefore, it can be said, that it is difficult to come up with a standard form of reality because we all vary with how we see the world, and how we live our lives. In simple terms, reality is an idea.

Reality is not the opposite of illusion rather the opposite of fake, and these fakes have little or no value, and should not be trusted and believed in.

Does reality exists mentally, or is it the physical world with all the people, buildings, and landscapes. Well, it is both. With this, it is important to understand the nature of reality and that it basically has two types.

- **Physical Reality (Material)**

  This is everything that is covered by the physical law, which uses our senses to interact with the physical world.

  But not everything physical is within the domain of our five senses. For example, we know gravity exists, and it's the reason we don't float around each other, still, we can't touch it. We just know it's there, whether we see it or not.

  Physical reality, aside from our senses, is based on our consciousness. So, as long as it is perceived by consciousness, it is physical reality, even if it doesn't fall under the domain of the senses.

- **Non-Physical Reality (Immaterial)**

  Non-physical reality is beyond the explanations of the physical law. These are the things that we know are real, but we cannot experience directly through our five senses.

The easiest example of a non-physical reality is your aliveness. If you are reading this, then you know you're alive, and that is the fact, and you wouldn't think otherwise.

But aliveness does not fall under the five senses and is beyond the explanations of the physical law. In physical law, aliveness would simply be explained as being animated, being able to grow, and being able to carry out the functions of a living body. But in non-physical reality, aliveness is broad and formless.

Non-physical reality is deep and abstract. The only way we could experience it is through our mind, where we can be free from the hustle and bustle of the physical world.

Physical reality and non-physical reality are not separate realities. Instead, they are interconnected. How we see the physical world, what we do in it, reflects so much of the state of our non-physical reality. Non-physical reality would transpire as physical reality.

You as a person are both physical and non-physical. In physical reality, you are how you appear to be, and how you behave in society. But in non-physical reality, you are how you truly perceive yourself to be. Your non-physical reality is translated into your physical reality, thus forming your personality.

> *"Life is a series of natural and spontaneous changes.*
> *Don't resist them; that only creates sorrow.*
> *Let reality be reality.*
> *Let things flow naturally forward*
> *In whatever way they like."*
> **~ Lao Tzu**

> *"Reality exists in the human mind, and nowhere else."*
> **~ George Orwell, 1984**

"First comes thought; then organization of that thought into ideas and plans; then transformation of those plans into reality. The beginning, as you will observe, is in your imagination."
~ Napoleon Hill

2. What is the purpose of life?

This is got to be one of the hardest questions to answer. Aristotle once discussed the purpose of life in his "Ergon Theory". The word "Ergon" in Greek means "function" or "job" or "skill".

Human beings and even objects have some sort of Ergon, a purpose behind why live or why they were built. According to Aristotle, the purpose of life to make the most out of your "Ergon" and do the best function you can which in Greek is called "arête".

For example:

- The purpose of a chair is to sit on it and it has to be soft, made sturdy and comfortable so it can continue its function for a long time.
- The purpose of a plastic bag is to contain items you buy at a grocery store or at the mall so it has to do a great job by not ripping or by not having holes to keep the items inside it in tack.

It's also the same with people. We have to do our "Ergon" (function), and make the most out of it by applying "arête" (expertise).

- The purpose of a doctor is to heal the sick and to do his "Ergon" effectively, he has to study well for so many years and master his field. A doctor knows that someone might die if he doesn't do his job well enough.

With everything that has been cited, the purpose of life is to carry out our functions in the best way we can. Therefore, everything that we do must be in line with that purpose.

We have many purposes in life, not only one. You can be a child, a student, a teacher, a sales lady at the department store, a parent with kids, a lawyer, a bus driver, etc., but the concept of doing the best in what you do remains the same for all of us.

Imagine the kind of society we have if everybody works on their job and tasks efficiently. We would all be very productive.

3. The Nature of Man

Man is composed of a "body" and a "soul". The body is the material component, and the soul is the spiritual component. It is not to be viewed "body + soul", because this would make man two individuals. Rather it means a body that is what it is, by reason of its union with the soul.

In Plato's ideas, the soul is the spirit which uses the body, as a sort of vessel. In his view, known as the "Platonic soul" man is composed of (1) mind/reason, (2) ego or emotion, and (3) appetite.

> *"It's not enough to have lived.*
> *We should be determined to live for something."*
> **~ Winston S. Churchill**

> *"If you can't figure out your purpose,*
> *figure out your passion."*
> *For your passion will lead you right into your purpose."*
> **~ Bishop T.D. Jakes**

> *"The soul which has no fixed purpose in life is lost; To*
> *be everywhere, is to be nowhere."*
> **~ Michel de Montaigne**

4. The Self

Plato gave two faculties of the human self: reason and desires.

- Reason is the one making judgments, using wisdom to reflect upon the world.
- Desires are dictated by our wants and senses.

5. What does it mean to have a good life?

To have a pretty good life is what we are striving for. This is one of the reasons why our parents or guardians send you off to school – so you can learn and hopefully one day, graduate and get the job of your dreams. This is also one of the reasons why parents work so hard, some even have more than one job – to provide food on the table, buy what you need, and take you to places.

But what is a good life? This is not a simple question for the answer may differ from one person to another.

Imagine two different people, sick, and lying on their deathbed, surrounded by their family and friends.

Man 1:

Adam is the CEO of a big marketing company. He lives in a two-story mansion, well-furnished, and fully installed with all the latest technology. He owns two luxury cars, which include a Porsche, which he uses to drive himself to work.

He has a lot of maids and workers who do all the work for him, so he can focus on running his company. With this, we can say, "He has lived a good life".

But Adam was never married and didn't have kids. He became CEO of the company after his parents died of a plane crash when he was young. Since then, he has lived with his maids, drivers, and his five pet dogs.

Knowing this story, other people might say, "Poor Adam, he has lived an awful life." There are two answers as to whether Adam did live a good life or not? Who is correct? Did Adam live a good life or not?

Man 2:

Paul is a painter, and to get inspiration for his artworks, he chose to buy a wooden house in the countryside, facing the hills and mountains.

Whenever he finishes ten paintings, he drives to the city, in his worn-out truck to sell what he could. He also accepts public art projects when there's an offer. Some people might say, "Poor Paul, he didn't even get the change to live a good life."

But Paul had a beautiful wife, a son, and a daughter. His son grew up to be a painter as himself, and his daughter became a local school teacher. His children already have kids of their own. Every Saturday, his children would come over to his house, with his grandchildren, and they would have a family dinner.

Knowing this story, other people might say, "It was simple, but he lived a good life."

The examples are two people with different social status. It means that having a good life is not based on tangible, material objects. We would be hypocrites if we say having a nice house, luxury items and people to things for us is not the "good life". It is for some people but it is not true for all. Some people define a good life like the second example, living a peaceful life free with all the hullabaloos of city life.

This means a "good life" is how we define it. We give meaning to it because we differ in what we value, and we have different goals and sources of happiness. You have the ability to live a good life and only you can tell whether your life is good - not other people. Therefore, there is no standard answer to the question, "What do you mean by having a good life?"

"The purpose of our lives is to be happy."
~ **Dalai Lama**

"Sing like no one's listening
Love like you've never been hurt
Dance like nobody's watching
And live like it's heaven on earth."
~**Mark Twain**

"Life is really simple
But men insist on making it complicated."
~ **Confucius**

B. Ethics

Ethics answers the question, "What should I do?" The word, ethics, comes from the Greek word, ***"ethos"***, which means, ***"character"***, or ***"custom"***. It is the study of morality or the idea of what is good and what is bad. Ethics is the ***"philosophy of life"*** and is sometimes referred to as ***"moral philosophy"***.

The study of ethics focuses mainly on the morality of human behaviors, whether what you are doing is right or wrong. Because man has ***"free will"***, he is the master of himself, and all his actions are done voluntarily, and with his own consent. So, it's important that human action is guided with ethics. Without ethics, our actions will be aimless or will have no direction.

For Example: *Luis randomly throws a rock and it flew over the fence. Unfortunately, he hits a boy just passing by.*

Who's to blame?

The blame will not fall on the rock, even if, technically, it is what hit the boy.

The blame should fall on the Luis, because he was one who conscientiously threw the rock over the fence, which hit the boy. Luis made the decision, not the non-living rock.

Ethics vs. Logic

Logic   -   science of right thinking

Ethics   -   science of right living

The most likely difference between them is that ethics is the study of principles with respect to right and wrong conduct while logic is a way of human thought that involves thinking in a straight, step-by-step manner about how a problem can be solved, logic is the bedrock of many principles including the scientific method.

When we say that someone argues in an ethical way, do we mean that they follow the rules of logic and logical reasoning? If all people were to stand by logic, would their arguments not also be ethical? Not all the time, the rules of logical reasoning do not imply ethical argument. The statement that logical argument equals ethical argument, while it may be mostly true, is not always, or totally true. Of course, you will be reported as unethical if you intentionally break the rules of an argument. But you can follow the rules of logic and still mislead or deceive your listeners.

Ethics vs. Psychology

Psychology -   studies how people behave and the reasons behind their behavior

Ethics   -   studies how people should and ought to behave in the society

Psychology considers individual differences and variations. Instead of studying the entire entity as it is, it separates individual variables based on human behavior. Despite the fact that psychology has its scale of ethics and morality, its aim is not to discuss what moral is or not, rather it is interested in what different morals exist.

Norms of Morality

Morality is based on doing what's right and what's wrong. We know about this now. But as a natural philosopher, questions that might pop are:

"How do you know if an action is right or wrong?"

"Is there a criteria or mechanics we can use to validate if an action is right or wrong?"

"Who judges whether an action is right or wrong?"

"What if an action is right for one person but is wrong for another? Who is right now, and who is wrong?"

Could young people be credible judges of morality?"

If you're thinking of these questions, you're thinking like a philosopher. Yes, that's right! To determine whether an action is right wrong, there has to be a certain basis, and that basis should not be merely opinionated. There should be a standard.

We call this standard, "Norms of Morality". A norm is a set of rules followed by the society but is not written in any law in any government.

For Example: *You should offer your seat to an old lady standing in the bus.*

This seems to be the most suitable thing to do, right?

If you do offer your seat to the old lady, you'll be seen as very considerate and respectful of the elderly.

But if you don't, you might feel bad about it. Worse, if a lot of people are looking at your direction, and saw you neglect the old lady, they might raise their eyebrows and look at you as if you're the most awful person on the bus.

There is an expected action for the situation. But there is no written rule in the law which states, "If you see an older person standing in the bus, offer your seat."

This is how the norms of morality work. It serves as the guide or standard of ethics.

Ethics accepts that man does what he pleases and acts according to his free will, which he has full control over.

"A man without ethics is a wild beast loosed upon this world."
~ Adams Camus, French Novelist

If ethics is practiced by everybody, the world could be a better place to live since we would always consider if what we're about to do is right or wrong, and how it would affect others. It also encourages better understanding between people, no matter the differences in age, race, color, social status, and culture.

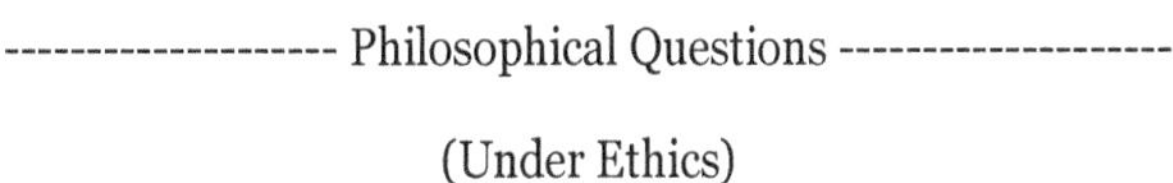

-------------------- Philosophical Questions --------------------

(Under Ethics)

1. What is free will?

    Various philosophers had many takes on the nature of our free will. Let's by classifying a person's action, of which it is subjective to his own free will.

    There are two (2) classifications of action, according to Aristotle's Nicomachean ethics.

    - Involuntary – actions that are carried out by the doer with or without his knowledge out of either (1) compulsion or (2) ignorance, while being aware or unaware of the possible consequences

- ✓ **Under Compulsion** – being forced to do an action making it difficult or even impossible to resist, which brings pain to its doer

  - ✓ **Through Ignorance** – when the doer of the action does not fully understand the circumstances, so decides upon it without much consideration

- Voluntary – actions that can be manipulated or decided upon by the doer, with the knowledge of the particular circumstances of the action and its consequences, may it be good or bad

  - ✓ **Cleary Voluntary** – the doer is fully aware of all possible options and the consequences of each options and decides upon the action with complete responsibility

  - ✓ **Non-Voluntary** – when the doer chose to carry out the action but out of ignorance, not even knowing how ignorant he is of the matter, which causes him pain and regret afterwards and makes him feel sorry about his action

  - ✓ **Under Compulsion** – decided upon by the doer but not fully out of self-choice, but of external influence which gave him alternatives to choose from; it's different from a compulsive involuntarily action because the doer is left with a choice, while there is none for the compulsive involuntary action, or just not realized by the doer at the time the action was carried out

"Free will is not the liberty to do whatever one likes
But the power of doing whatever one sees ought to be done
Even in the very face of otherwise overwhelming impulse.
There lies freedom, indeed."
~ George Macdonald
"The forces of good and evil are working within and around me
I must choose, and in a free will universe
I do have a choice."
~ Martin Luther

2. What is virtue?

During his time, Plato laid the "Four Cardinal Virtues": moderation/temperance, courage, justice, and wisdom.

Also, in his "moral theory", he explained that the moral values are eternal, unchanging and non-physical. Furthermore, he stated that the "good", is the source of an ultimate moral perfection. This means that to have good life is to have a virtuous life.

3. What is true happiness?

Aristotle taught that happiness should not only be the "telos", or end goal of all human action but should be the aim of all human activities. He called happiness, *"eaudamonia"*.

Moreover, happiness can't be attained with virtues alone, rather it can be achieved through (1) moral goodness, (2) constant training, and (3) physical characteristics.

Although there are three, virtue is the most important aspect and serves as the distinguishing factor between man and animal.

"Happiness consists more in conveniences of pleasure
That occurs everyday
Than in great pieces of good fortune
That happen but seldom."
~ Benjamin Franklin

"Happiness is not something ready-made.
It comes from your own actions."
~ Dulai Lama

"The essence of philosophy is that a man should so live
That his happiness shall depend as little as possible
on external things."
~ Epictetus

4. What is friendship?

Friendship is one of the central topics of ancient philosophy, and up to this date, it is one of the most essential elements of a healthy and ideal society. Basically, friendship is a form of intimacy of one person to two or more persons, which is grounded on genuine love and concern, for one another.

Our friends deeply affect our attitude and personality both negatively and positively. Hence the saying, "tell me who your friends are, and I'll tell you who you are". Here are some ways your friends affect you as a person.

- Friends affect the way you feel about yourself.

    It's normal that to stay friends, you would seek the approval of your circle of friends. But even in a group of friends, there are different degrees of personality, and normally, there is a person with a stronger personality than the rest, and there are those who are sometimes pushed behind, even without them knowing it. This might take a toll on you, as you could feel inferior about yourself.

But a good friendship can identify one may not be as strong as the other. So instead of pushing them down, pull them up and assure them than they are accepted, flaws and all.

- Friends affect the way you think, talk, and behave.

Friendship is one of the three types of love, established by ancient Greek philosophers and stated in the Bible. It is grounded on love, understanding, concern, support, and mutual caring. Next to family, a friend is probably the most important person to you.

The three types of love are (1) agape, (2) eros, and (3) philia. Friendship falls under *"Agape"*, the love for other people, in general, outside our family. Friendship is a mutual and positive attitude between two or more individuals. For Aristotle, friendship can be considered as a form of virtue because it helps or ought to help each friend improve and feel accepted in the friendship.

If you are always with your friends, which is very likely, especially nowadays, you also acquire or adapt to their likes and dislikes.

That's why friendship often comes as cliques. Cliques are groups with the same interest and hang out with each other because they relate with one another. You think alike, you talk alike, act alike, and even dress alike. That's why you prefer each other's company.

For example, at school, we give names to groups such as:

• **"The Nerds" or "The Smarties"** – those who consistently pull off good grades and are often pictured out with glasses and braces

• **"The Jocks"** – the school varsity players who often carry around a basketball, and wear varsity jackets, even under the scorching sun

- **"The Cool Kids"** – often times the rich kids, who are very popular in campus, at the same time, affluent and attractive, and are oftentimes well-liked; they are very likely to win school elections

- **"The Good-ats"** – these are the school achievers who often represent the school in various competitions, and actually bring home the bacon; they excel in a multitude of extracurricular activities and have their faces printed in tarpaulins

- **"The Campus Crush"** – the prettiest, most handsome faces who usually hang out together, and thus get a lot of attention at school

- **"The Ethnic Groups"** – students from other races or ethnicities; the foreign students

- **"The Singers"** – these are the musically inclined who often sing inside the classroom and along the hallways, and bring their guitars and beat boxes with them anywhere

- **"The Ottaku"** – the anime and manga lovers who always wear shirts with their favorite characters.

- **"The Gamers"** – online games are such a thing now and these gamers are often in front of their gadget having duels or multiple battles

- **"The Bookworms"** – they are sometimes called "The Loners", because they are quite passive and silent and prefers the company of books and people who also love good reads

According to Aristotle's Nicomachean Ethics, there are three types of friendship.

- **Friends for Pleasure** – these are friends you enjoy bonding with during your spare time – people who want you around in parties, going to the mall, eating out, playing sports or games, and movie marathons. But outside these activities, they might not have any communication with you.

- **Friends for Benefits** – these are friends who often seek you out when they need help with their school projects, or borrow something from you – but after doing them favors and giving them what they're asking for, they don't have much interaction with you

- **Friends for Goodness or True Friends** – in Aristotle's words, true friends are "a single soul dwelling in two bodies"; these are friends who, even without the pleasure and benefit, stick with you, and enjoy your company, even if that means silence; these are also your friends who seem to feel when you're okay and when you're not like you are connected

- Friends affect you physical and mental health.

It's important to choose your friends carefully because they have a great impact on your health. When you are in good terms with your friends, you tend to be happier and more energetic and build a more active and outdoor lifestyle.

But, when friendship turns into conflict, it also affects you emotionally. When friends fight, one might feel unaccepted, or rejected, and even depressed if it prolongs.

"A sweet friendship refreshes the soul."
~ *Proverbs 27:9 (Bible)*

"The glory of friendship is not the outstretched hand, not the kindly smile, nor the joy of companionship; it is the spiritual inspiration that comes to one when you discover that someone else believes in you and is willing to trust you with a friendship."

~ Ralph Waldo Emerson

"A friend is one that knows you as you are, understands
where you have been, accepts what you have become, and
still, gently allows you to grow."
*~ **William Shakespeare***

5. What is evil?

The concept of "evil" is commonly associated with religion and belief, but it can also be explained without touching our religious differences. Is evil real? Why is there evil in the world? Yes, evil does exist and so, we need to understand its nature. The problems of evil are subjects under theology and ethics.

Although we despise evil as it is, in a way, it helps us separate evil from non-evil, the good and bad. Without evil, there is no sense of comparison. Thomas Aquinas argued that there are two types of evil:

- **Natural Evil** – evil not cause by man but by natural causes, which man cannot control, which bring pain and suffering to people; this includes natural calamities (earthquakes, typhoons, tsunamis, floods, famines, diseases, accidents, sickness, and injuries)

- **Moral Evil** – evil caused by man, intentional or by choice, not by natural causes, which bring pain and suffering to people; this includes wars, conflicts, crimes, assaults, etc.

On the other hand, Aristotle also had his take on evil. He explained three types of evil.

- **Vice** – character of attitude which is either an excess or a deficiency of virtue; the excess of vice was called *"rashness"*, and the deficiency was called "cowardice"; although in the modern day, we understand vices as excessive and unhealthy habits such as smoking, drinking alcohol, gambling, and the likes

- **Incontinence** – lack of self-control over things under pleasure, satisfaction, and self-indulgence; not being contented with what you have that would make you crave for more and do everything to have more; when this concept is applied to eating more than what you need or capable of, it is called "gluttony"

- **Brutality** – considered to be irrational and an extreme type of evil which brings harm not only to the doer of the action but, to everything around him

But since we do not have control over natural evil, we should focus on correcting moral evil. Like aforementioned, moral evil is brought by the choice of its doer. We can connect this to the existence of our free will, having the choice to do what we think is right or wrong.

Free will can be one of the reasons behind the existence of evil.

- ✓ Man decides to bully and hurt other people.
- ✓ Man decides to practice "crab mentality", the act of pulling each other down, like crabs fighting over a spot on top of a rock.
- ✓ Man decides to laugh at other people's flaws.
- ✓ Man decides to commit murder, robbery, and physical violence.
- ✓ Man decides to indulge in vices despite the health risk and financial consequences.
- ✓ Man decides to lie, and white lies are still considered lies.
- ✓ Man decides to gossip about other people's live and spread false accusations.
- ✓ Man decides to disrespect their parents and the elderlies.

Free will should be practiced with responsibility and moral considerations.

> *"The world is a dangerous place to live*
> *Not because of the people who are evil*
> *But because of the people who don't do anything about it."*
> *~ **Albert Einstein***

> *It is a man's own mind, not his enemy or foe*
> *That lures him to evil ways.*
> *~ **Buddha***

> *Evil communication corrupts good manners.*

C. Epistemology

Epistemology answers the question, "How do we know what we know?" and "What is knowledge?" It comes from the Greek words, ***"episteme"*** meaning "knowledge", and ***"logos"*** meaning "study or explanation of". Epistemology literally means, the ***"philosophical study of knowledge"***.

It is concerned with everything about knowledge, the sources of knowledge, its criteria, how we gain it, and its limitations, if there are. It has three essential elements: belief, truth, and justification.

Knowledge comes from a certain "belief", which was studied and validated to be true. There are two types of knowledge or belief.

- ***a priori*** - or non-empirical knowledge; means ***"from before"*** in Latin; "a priori" is the knowledge and belief from before any investigation, experimentation, or experience, and uses only reason

  For Example: *Abstract claims*

  Knowledge of Logical Truths

- ***a posteriori*** - or empirical knowledge; means ***"from after"*** in Latin; "a posteriori" is the knowledge and belief acquired after investigation, experimentation, or sensory experience, combined with the use of reason

  For Example: *Knowledge of the locations of various countries under the seven continents of the world*

  Basketball ball, stress ball, apples and oranges, are round. You know these statements are true because you have
seen and touched these objects.

Epistemology Schools of Thought

1. Rationalism

Rationalism argues that the significant way to gain knowledge about the world is through "reason" and is independent of sense experience, contrary to the belief of empiricism. This is why rationalism and empiricism has been in conflict with each other.

Rationalists believe that reason is superior to sense experience, and that even without sense experience, knowledge can be achieved. In addition to reason, rationalism also believes in proof or evidence that supports and justifies the knowledge, otherwise it cannot be accepted as true.

2. Empiricism

Empiricism explains that the ultimate way to achieve knowledge is through "sense experience", and not reason alone, as taught in rationalism. Empiricism explained that reason can only expound on the relationship of one idea to another, so in order to gain a complete understanding of these ideas, they have to be experienced.

If an idea can't be experienced by the senses, then it can be considered as "unknown".

Empiricism has been in contrast with rationalism metaphysics in general, since metaphysical knowledge deals with everything beyond sense experience.

3. Skepticism

By definition, skepticism means being doubtful, or questioning the truth behind a certain knowledge. It is having the human mind's natural questioning attitude. In philosophy, a question is more commonly called "inquiry". Skepticism is the belief that some, if not all, knowledge is impossible to gain.

This means than it doesn't mean an idea was justified with reason, it can be accepted true. Therefore, if the reasoning is poor, it is better to be skeptic (doubtful) about it, and suspend the belief.

In a way, skepticism is quite healthy because it filters the knowledge presented to us, and tells us that not all ideas should be easily believed on. But there are extreme skeptics who believe that all knowledge is impossible and that even reality is questionable.

4. Dogmatism

The simplest way to help you understand dogmatism is to define it as the "I am right" way of thinking in which a dogmatic person has many beliefs and ideas in his minds and he would never question them no matter what.

He would believe his own ideas to be true, and does everything to protect them, justify them, and uphold them, persuading others to believe like them.

When another person tries to disprove his "dogmas", they would do everything to prove his right. It's a certain confidence and assertiveness to one's personal beliefs and opinions.

-------------------- Philosophical Questions --------------------

(Under Epistemology)

What is Knowledge?

Knowledge is the understanding of the realities of our world. It can also be defined as a "justified true belief", since it comprises of the same three words.

> *"To attain knowledge, add things everyday.*
> *To attain wisdom, remove things every day."*
> *~ **Lao Tzu***

D. Logic

Logic comes from the Greek word, ***"logos"***, which originally means, "word" or ***"what is spoken"***.

Logic is the science of proper reasoning and deals with arguments, by observation and experimentation. Moreover, it allows us to distinguish good arguments from bad arguments and decide whether to further pursue or withdraw. You should learn how to reason effectively so you can convince others to do something or believe in what you believe in.

For example, you are asking your parents to buy you a new phone but they seem to be unsure. You can consider researching about the phone you like and using this essential information to convince your parents that the features of this phone would benefit you a lot. The stronger your logic and reasoning is, the more convincing you'll be. Your parents would finally say "yes", to that brand new phone.

Two Types of Logic

Logic has two types.

- **Deductive** – also called **"top-bottom logic"**, and starts with a general statement, and uses this to think of specific details or examples, and then coming up with a conclusion

  Example: *"Mammals produce milk for their babies."*

  You know of this because it is taught in schools. This is true.

You saw little kittens and puppies suck milk from their mothers. Therefore, you conclude, that "cats and dogs are both mammals".

On the other hand, you never saw a chicken feed her chicks with milk. So, unlike cats and dogs, chickens aren't mammals.

What are they?

"Birds have feathers."

This is another idea you learned from school.

"Chickens have feathers, even if they can't fly. So, if chickens aren't mammals, they must be birds."

- **Inductive** – also called, **"bottom-up logic"**, and looks at the specific details or examples to come up with your own conclusion

  Example: *Your friend's birthday is next week. You're planning to buy him a shirt. You know he would love a shirt with any of the "Avengers" characters on it. You also know he's a medium size.*

  The problem is, you don't know what color to buy.

  You notice that your friend's backpack is color blue, as well as his lunch box, his shoes, and his cellphone case.

  You come up with a general conclusion that, "Oh, his favorite color must be blue."

  Although you aren't exactly sure that this is true because you never asked him what his favorite color is.

  But you become confident enough to buy your friend a blue Avenger shirt, since most of his stuffs are of that color.

Basically, logic has certain principles which guide our reasoning. Most commonly applied principle is the one that deals with the conditional clause "if-then,...is" There are several of such principles, but the main (not the only) thing that we is looked into in logic are principles governing the authenticity of arguments , in other words, it checks whether specific conclusions adhere to some given assumptions. For instance, let's take a look at these arguments :

If Tom is a boy, then Tom likes Ben10

Tom is a boy. Therefore, Tom likes Ben10

If X is greater than 10, then X is greater than 2.

X is greater than 10, therefore, X is greater than two.

If an animal has feather, then the animal is a bird.

Fowls have feathers, therefore, fowls are birds.

If an animal produces milk, then it is a mammal

Fowls do not produce milk, therefore, fowls are not mammals

These instances are clearly good arguments in the sense that their conclusions follow from the assumptions. If the assumptions of the argument appear to be true, the conclusion of the argument must also be true. This form of argument in logic is referred to as"modus ponens" :

If P, then Q.

P. Therefore Q

-------------------- Philosophical Questions --------------------

(Under Logic)

- Is argument is the best way to discuss with those who oppose the truth?

When we wish to correct people with clear reasons we are sure of and to show the other party that they're wrong, we must handle things from what side that they view the matter, for it might turn out to be true from their side, and admit that truth to them, but reveal to the other party the side on which it is false. The other party might probably be satisfied with that, for he sees that he was not mistaken, and that he only failed to see all sides. Now, no one is offended when they're told they're not seeing everything because no one does; but one does not like to be mistaken, and that perhaps arises from the fact that man naturally cannot see everything, and that naturally he cannot be wrong in the side he looks at, since the opinions of your senses are always true.

So, Pascal is of the opinion that a direct strategy may not correct with correct opinion, that is why I think he recommended admitting first that the "opposer" was heard and was understood, which is the first truth, then inputting the idea logically through the backdoor of their beliefs, looking for a different angle that is revealing to him, thus, a side on which that "first truth" is false.

People are generally better convinced by the reasons which they have themselves discovered than by those which have come into the mind of others.

Furthermore, arguing may bring in the ego, which is not logical and may tend to strengthen the views of a truth-denier. This is probably because people tend to be convinced better by their own-found arguments, from the angle that they see and there are many angles to every question.

- Is rationality a standard?

Rationality is a complex set up. Rationality includes logical views and avoiding frequent errors, but it also involves judgements where the rational agent is trying to uncover truths or at least be sufficiently right to increase chances of survival. It is tempting to say that logical agent will always try to follow a strategy to achieve some objectives. That may be true, but being logical requires more by requiring the agent to assess evidence in support of or against a judgement in a way that is verifiable by another rational agent. I think that the requirement of evidence assessment is reasonable, otherwise the rational agent could end up supporting a judgement that is not supported by evidence at all. But judgement is often a matter of likelihood, and theories emerge when accounting for the evidence which do not meet the currently accepted norms for acceptance. Thus rationality is subject to the imposition of norms, but the norms themselves need to be adaptable to revision in the light of new evidence and new theories which account for that evidence.

- In which case will we be the most ready to expect the unexpected and why?

Expecting the unexpected" is just a paradoxical way of saying "we have no certain expectation of what is to come" or " we do not know what to expect". This can happen, at different and every point in our lives as human beings, it could be the unexpected death of a family member who has been slightly ill, and then family disputes over will, it could be in form of postponement of examination or test prior to a strike or any unforeseen incident. So we expect this unexpected thing to happen.

E. Aesthetics

Aesthetics is the study of "art, beauty, and expression". It comes from the Greek word, ***"aesthetikos"*** which means "the one who is perceptive of things through his sensations, feelings, and intuitions". It is concerned with the purpose of art, what it consists of, its nature, forms, and a person's personal taste and appreciation. It also answers the question, "What makes something beautiful?"

Art is as old as human history. We all have a unique form of art inside of us because art has is "abstract", and has no definite form.

When we see a work of art, the most cliché reaction would be, "That is beautiful". But art is more than just appreciating the beauty in it. Art is how we express it its artistry and beauty, delving deeper into its meaning.

It is the reflection of the way we think as an individual. Art is not only a form of recreation, and is not restricted to paintings, drawings, sculptures, and everything you can find in a museum during an educational trip.

It's definitely more than that! Art is a creative way of interpreting one's view of reality. Therefore, aesthetics can be defined also, as the study of sensory values

-------------------- Philosophical Questions --------------------

(Under Aesthetics)

- Can beauty be measured?

Every human society that has ever existed has developed standards for judging works of art,music, and poetry as better than or worse than... This tells us that the fact that there is no precise mathematical method for doing this does not mean that there is no measure at all. The real issue is how is it then possible to measure, if there is no standard agreed worldwide.

There have been art exhibition, music competitions, beauty contests since time immemorial and all these have required judging each of these works of art. But what is being measured is not an objective standard that looks the same to everyone like meters and kilos, but subjective relationships between the observer and what is being observed. So, though we are all genetically similar, and it is likely that sweet foods hold a greater appeal to most than sour foods, some still prefer the sour food, probably due to one reason or the other. There is something we share in our minds that guarantees most will prefer to decorate their tables with roses rather than radishes, but a few, may still go ahead to choose the radish.

Even in things we do everyday, selecting the most beautiful dress, selecting the most beautiful girl, selecting the student with the best handwriting, that is us measuring aesthetics.

- Can an object of art lack aesthetic properties?
Conceptual Art "is not meant to be looked at aesthetically, but to be thought about intellectually." — **Phaidon's The Art Museum**

Thinking intellectually about a work of art can still involve aesthetic point of views, whether positive or negative. However, there may be borderline cases. Does a conceptual piece consisting simply of a card on a gallery wall and bearing only a title and an artist's name have aesthetic properties? Arguably, any aesthetic properties would lie entirely in the ideas behind it rather than the object on the wall itself, so the aesthetic properties would be like those of literature rather than visual art. Alternatively, some would demur from regarding the card as an art object at all.

- Can an art object fail to elicit an aesthetic response?

Yes, but not because it lacks the potential to do so. An aesthetic response is an emotional response caused directly through the senses. The intellect does not intervene. One can experience the beauty, ugliness, normalcy, transformation, etc. in something without consciously thinking about what one is perceiving and why. Anything perceptible, by definition, has the potential to cause an aesthetic response. Aesthetic responses can be described and analysed to determine what principles they appear to follow. However, these principles do not belong to the object as its aesthetic; an aesthetic is not a property in that sense, what gives the aesthetic property is the mental notion a piece of art gives you.

F. Axiology

The word **_"axiology"_** comes from the Greek word **_"axios"_** meaning "worthy" and **_"logos"_** meaning "to study". Literally, axiology is the study of value or what has worth for man.

Axiology is the study of values and how those values are brought about in a society. Axiology seeks to understand the nature of values and the judgments of values. It is closely related to two other concepts of philosophy which are ethics and aesthetics. All these three concepts deal with "Worth". Ethics is concerned with goodness, trying to understand the difference between what good is and what it means to be good. Aesthetics on its own end, deals with beauty and harmony, trying to understand beauty and what it means or how it is defined. Axiology is an important component of both ethics and aesthetics, because one must use concepts of worth to define "goodness" or "beauty," and therefore one must understand what is valuable and why such a thing is valuable. Understanding values helps us to determine the motive behind a particular action.

When you ask your parents questions like "why should I do this?" or "why should I not do this?" you are asking axiological questions. You want to find out what it is that causes you to take such actions or refrain from such actions. For instance, your mum tells you not to take a cookie from the jar, and you keep wondering why taking a cookie from the jar is wrong and you question your mum. In return, your mum who is tired of trying to explain and simply replies, "Because I said so." The child will stop arguing if he values the established authority or if he fears the punishment of disobeying. On the other hand, the child may stop arguing simply because he respects his mum. In this example, the value is either authority or respect, depending on the values of the child. Axiology asks, "Where did these values come from? Can either of these values be called good? Is one better than another? If so, Why is one better than the other?" "How is one better than the other?" Axiology is said to be primarily concerned with classifying what things are good, and how good they are. The axiology theory is also referred to as the theory of value, value means the worth of a thing. But in a more useful sense, "value theory" designates the area of moral philosophy that is concerned with specific questions about value and goodness of all varieties.

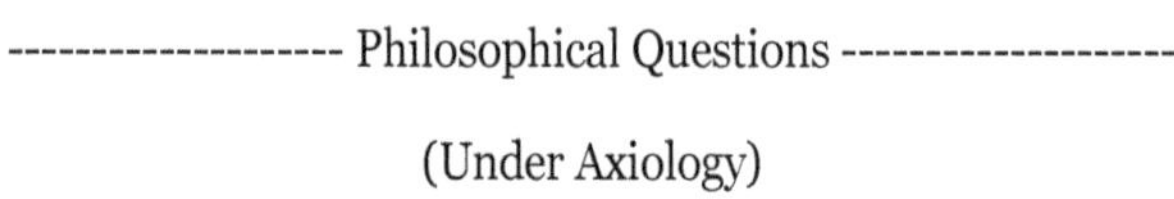

-------------------- Philosophical Questions --------------------

(Under Axiology)

- Why is equality assumed to be good?

It's perfectly clear that human beings are not equal in every aspect, if you take five minutes walk down the street, you'll understand better. You see a child who's so gifted and talented, does everything well, brilliant, athletic, cute, happy home and right in that same class you might find a student who is still struggling to get the first topic they were taught, looking dull, shy, can't even speak properly, hardly does things right, in our society there's the rich and there's the poor, and so on. We actually get to see that equality doesn't exist naturally, because while some people are naturally advantageous, some are naturally lagging behind. Therefore, what the law tends to do is to place everyone on a neutral and equal scale, where each one has equal opportunities, equal resources and equal rights. Even though the law tries to bring in that part that nature didn't provide us with, it is not entirely achievable yet. Then, since we have no way to neutrally measure people's worth in advance it seems appropriate to give them all equal opportunities.

- If something is fake, does that mean it is bad?

Mostly, yes but not always. Most of the time, the item may serve the expected purpose for a reasonable amount of time, but its quality as well as the quality of what it does, might not beat the original item.

The term "Fake" makes a judgement on type that is: if all the relevant property types of an object do not have the same value, measurement, or description of a standard example, then the object is fake only if it is presented as a lesser valued version of the standard example. We tend to have developed an innate biased mind that assumes fake means bad maybe because of what we have experienced in many instances of fake goods being of lesser value, but that doesn't make it all generally bad. For instance, if a friend of yours gifts you with a Manchester United's jersey, you are very much aware that the only original jersey is the one produced by the club's jersey manufacturer. However, the fact that the jersey you are gifted isn't the original one doesn't mean it's bad.

G. Political Philosophy

Political philosophy is the study of "good governance" and tells us how we should behave in a society, with ethics being one of the main considerations. It argues that man is naturally political and that our society is always connected to politics.

Two important questions under political philosophy are, "Who should rule?" and "What is the ideal society".

Political philosophy also attempts to come up with an ideal society and implements rules that people must follow, in order to achieve this.

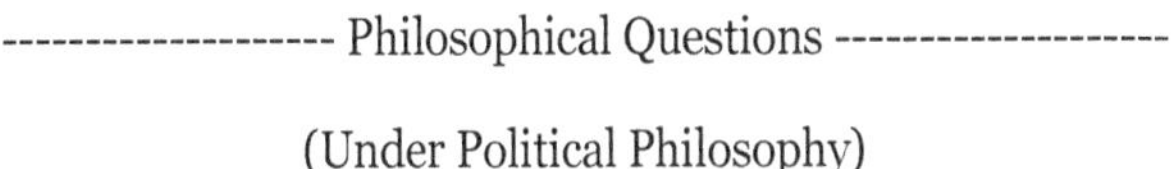

(Under Political Philosophy)

1. What is Freedom?

Freedom, generally, is being able to act or change without constraint. Something is "free" if it can change easily, and is not restricted in its present state. In philosophy, freedom is associated with having free will without undue or unnecessary constraints, or enslavement. Likewise, freedom is an idea firmly related to the concept of liberty. Freedom as one of the main philosophical categories describes the essence of man and his existence. Therefore, the meaningful definition of freedom is something of this kind in us that does not depend on us, in other words, freedom is "your own will, your way of seeing things, your ability to act in a way that's devoid of restraint, bondage, slavery, subjection to the will of others". If we're to be more detailed, freedom would be seen as a person's potential ability to freely choose an alternative, for instance, an opportunity to think and act following ideas, plans and desires, and this opportunity should not be because of internal or external coercion.

Also, Freedom is a state of mind; it is a philosophical concept that shows basic human option to understand one's human will. Outside of freedom, a person cannot understand and explore the abundance of his inner world and his capabilities. Freedom starts to end precisely where a person purposely restricts himself. Therefore, freedom is a core universal value that most people are striving for, because only in freedom and through freedom can the creative human potential be understood and achieved.

2. What are the Duties of a Citizen to His Country?

Political philosophy teaches that every citizen should be self-sufficient. Each individual has a function in the society, called the "social role", which can be accomplished successfully by being both knowledgeable and excellent in our respective function.

"Ask not what your country can do for you;
Ask what you can do for your country."
*~ **John F. Kennedy***

"It is not always the same thing to be a good man
and a good citizen."
*~ **Aristotle***

"No one is born a good citizen; No nation is born a democracy.
Rather, both are processes that continue to evolve over a lifetime.
Young people must be included from birth.
A society that cuts off from its youth severs its lifeline."
*~ **Kofi Annan***

3. Justice

According to Aristotle, justice is related to both lawfulness and fairness, in the execution of the law, executed by a just society. Justice is based on the law, and the law should be based on virtue.

For him, a just society is that which is composed of citizens who not only understand what is virtuous, but practices the virtues.

"Justice will not be served until those who are unaffected are as outraged as those who are."
~ Benjamin Franklin

"True peace is not merely the absence of war, it is the presence of justice".
~ Jane Addams

*The safety of the people requireth further from him
or them that have the sovereign power
That justice be equally administered to all degrees of people
That is, that as well the rich and mighty as poor
And obscure persons may be righted of the injuries done them."*
~ Thomas Hobbes

Chapter 4 – Famous Names in Philosophy and Their Contributions

In chapter 3, we learned about the different branches of philosophy, and the school of thought under each branch.

Chapter 4 is equally important. In this chapter, we will get to know the famous personalities behind the sayings and quotations we often read or heard of, and the reason behind them stating these lines.

It's important for us to know the contributions of the following people in philosophy because they are the same individuals responsible to the knowledge we of life and our world today. We simply owe it to them. At the same time, we can get inspiration from their stories, and possibly, bring out the philosopher in us.

A. Greek Philosophers

- Thales of Miletus (624 BC - 547 BC)
  Title: *"The First Western Philosopher", and "Father of Natural Philosophy"*
  Famous Line: *"Nothing is more active than thought, for it travels over the universe, and nothing is stronger than necessity for all must submit to it."*

  "The most difficult thing in life is to know yourself."

  Known for: Water as the Primary Principle

  Thales of Miletus was one of the "Seven Wise Men of Greece", or the **"Seven Sages"**.

  Thales of Miletus believed that the Earth floated on water and was made of the same materials as woods, which was observed to have floated on water too. Of course, you might say "That's ridiculous!" But during those times, the people believed that everything was created and preserved by the gods and goddesses of Greek mythology.

Because of questioning natural phenomena, Thales of Miletus became the "Father of Natural Philosophy".

Remarkable Works: *"On the Solstice", and "On the Equinox"*

- Pythagoras (570 BC - 495 BC)
  Title: *"Father of Numbers", and "The Samian Sage"*
  Famous Line: *"Be silent or let thy words be worth more than silence."*

  "Choose rather to be strong of soul than strong of body."

  "As long as Man continues to be the ruthless destroyer of lower living beings, he will never know health or peace. For as long as men massacre animals, they will kill each other. Indeed, he who sows the seed of murder and pain cannot reap joy and love."

Known for: Pythagoreanism

Pythagoras believed that the human soul is immortal meaning if we die, we will only continue living over and over again through a process called, **"reincarnation"** or rebirth, nation or rebirth, a belief which is similar to the teachings of Buddhism in Asian countries like China, and India.

Pythagoreanism was actually considered an underground cult, which was only revealed after the death of Pythagoras. His followers were called, "Pythagoreans". Their way of life included taking care of the body and the soul by having restrictions on food, to ensure the best possible reincarnation or "next life".

It's quite bizarre, but Pythagoreans didn't eat beans, and also meat, according to some sources. Are you okay with not eating beans? How about meat?

Pythagoras made many great contributions in Mathematics, although, he also emphasized that everything in the entire universe, including life, is dictated by numbers. We just didn't know the right formula to all of it yet. "Number rules the universe", as Pythagoras once said.

With this, he used odd numbers to represent men, and even numbers to represent women. Members of the so called cult prayed to **"Tetractys"**, the perfect equilateral triangle, and considered number "10" the supreme number.

Pythagoreanism has many followers. The larger outer circle was called **"Akousmatiko"**, and the inner circle, with whom Mathematical secrets were shared, was called **"Mathematikoi"**.

Remarkable Works: *"The Golden Verses", and "Imnurile Sacre"*

- Socrates (469 BC - 399 BC)
  Title: *"One of the Founders of Western Philosophy"*
  Famous Line: *"The only thing I know, is that I know nothing."*

  > *"To know, is to know that you know nothing. That is the meaning of true knowledge."*

  > *"Be kind, for everyone you meet is fighting a hard battle."*

Known for: Socratic Paradox

With this, Socrates teaches that it is okay to admit that you do not know everything. There are many things you still don't know.

Acknowledging and accepting the things you don't know are necessary in order to learn new things. It is like saying, "I want to know more". There is no shame to that.

The reason why only a few raises their hands during class recitations is because of fear of being ridiculed. You sometimes assume that you are the only one in class who do not know. So, you pretend you understand the lesson and don't ask questions.

But, who knows? You might not be the only one who has the same question in mind. How would you know the answer if you do not ask questions?

Socrates was sentenced to death by drinking a poison called "hemlock", for the crime of corrupting the minds of the youth, with his philosophical ideas.

Remarkable Works: *Socrates never wrote anything personally but several works written about him were "Apology", and Plato's "The Trial and Death of Socrates".*

- Democritus (460 BC - 370 BC)
  Title: *"The Laughing Philosopher"*
  Famous Line: *"Happiness resides not in possessions, and not in gold, happiness dwells in the soul."*

  "It is greed to do all the talking but not to want to listen at all."

  "Everything existing in the universe is the fruit of chance and necessity".

Known for: Atomism

Democritus believed that reality and everything is made up of particles that collided and fused together to produce more visible forms. If this was true, Democritus was in search of the smallest particle that makes up reality – the one particle which has started all forms and is invisible (being very small), and indivisible.

He called this particle, **"atomos"** which means **"undivided"** or **"indivisible"** in Greek. According to Democritus, the atomos were countless particles that move through the void (complete emptiness), and was the basic unit of reality. These atomos, or atoms as we called in the modern-day, collided with one another, to form an identifiable matter which can be seen.

Today, of course, we have been taught, that an atom is divisible and is not exactly the smallest particle, because atoms are still made up of protons, neutrons, and electrons.

Remarkable Works: *"Great World System" and "Little World System"*
(sometimes associated with Leucippus)

- Plato (427 BC - 347 BC)
  Title: *"Father of Idealism Philosophy"*
  Famous Line: *"Happiness depends upon ourselves."*

  "The beginning is the most important part of the work."

  "He who is not a good servant will not be a good master."

Known for: Theory of the Tripartite Soul

Even up to this day, Plato is one of the most influential philosophers of all time. Plato is a pupil of Socrates. Like those before him, he also believed in the immortality of the soul.

In his famous book, "The Republic", he defined the idea of the "tripartite soul", explaining that a person's soul is divided into three different parts.

- **Logistikon**
  Logical part; the part of our soul which has thoughts, rationality, and logic, and is capable of making wise, just, and reasonable decisions

- **Thymoeides**
  Spirited part; the part of our soul which makes us feel strong emotions like anger, jealousy, and envy, and should work together with "logistikon" , to maintain goodness

- **Epithymetikon**
  Appetitive part; the part of our soul which has appetites or desires for food, material things, money, power and more

Remarkable Works: *"The Republic", "Apology", and "Phaedo"*

- Aristotle (384 BC - 322 BC)
  Title: *"The Philosopher"*

Famous Line: *"It is the mark of an educated mind to be able to entertain a thought without accepting it."*

"There is only one way to avoid criticism: do nothing, say nothing, and be nothing."

"Educating the mind without educating the heart is no education at all."

Known for: The Doctrine of the Mean

Aristotle is said to have educated the son of Philip of Macedonia who was later known as Alexander the Great.

Aristotle contributed to several branches of philosophy, all of which made huge impacts even to how we understand it today.

One of his most famous teachings is the "doctrine of the mean". He stated that virtue lies on the mean. What do you mean by Aristotle's mean?

In our mathematics or statistics subjects, we were taught that the mean is the average, right? If we put it into philosophical concepts, the mean is the average basis of what is to be considered as a virtuous action. In Aristotle's explanation, there are three levels to it:

- Deficiency
- Virtue
- Excess

With virtue being the average action, which Aristotle called the "Golden Mean", anything beyond is an excess, and anything below is a deficiency, and both are to be considered not virtuous. This could be the origin of the saying, "live according to your means", which is living, consuming, or spending only what is needed and not deficient nor excessive.

Example: *You are given a budget of $20 per day because that is only what your parents are capable of providing you. You are instructed to budget* *your money to cover for your daily expenses at school such as food and transportation.*

To be virtuous is to spend only according to what your $20 can go. Going over the budget would be considered excessive already. Let's say you bought unnecessary stuff along the way even if you know you cannot afford it, and to do so, you are forced to borrow money from your friends just to buy things not exactly necessary for you to fulfill all your functions for the day.

On the other hand, depriving yourself too much of the things you need is a deficiency and is also considered not virtuous. Let's say for example, you skip your meals and go hungry for no valid reason, even if you can afford to buy a decent snack with your money.

The doctrine of the mean teaches us of the balance between what is less and what is too much in order to live a virtuous life.

Remarkable Works: *"Physics", "Ta Meta Ta Physika" (the books that comes after the book about "Physics", "Nicomachean Ethics about practical ethics")*

B. Western Philosophers

- Aurelius Augustinus or St. Augustine of Hippo (1225 – 1274)
  Nationality: Algerian
  Title: *"Most Significant Christian Theologian", "Doctor of the Church"*
  Famous Line: *"It was pride that changed angels into devils; it is humility that makes men as angels."*

  "Faith is to believe what you do not yet see; the reward for this faith is to see what you believe."

"Do you wish to rise? Begin by descending. You plan a tower that will pierce the clouds? Lay first the foundation of humility."

Known for: Manichaean Background and Doctrine of the Original Sin

Manichaeism and Augustine

Manichaeism was not founded by St. Augustine of Hippo, but he became one of its followers, for some time. Manichaeism started in Persia, founded by a religious leader named Mani. Being raised in North Africa at the zenith of Manichaeism, St. Augustine acquired its practices.

Manichaeism presented two principles – the principle of good, which pertained to light and was called *"Ormuzd"* (their god), and the bad principle, which was related to darkness or evil, and was called *"Ahriman"*. The believed the world is a continuous war between the Lord of Light and the Lord of Darkness.

Just like other philosophers, St. Augustine of Hippo believed that a person comprises of a body and a soul. He believed that the soul is pure and is a product of good principle but, the body can be composed and polluted by bad principles.

To keep the soul pure and good, Manichaeism taught abstaining from physical pleasure, including having intimate relationship and physical relationship with the opposite gender, and suggested activities that would people abstain from pleasure. They also didn't consume extravagant, rich food, like meat and wine, and were not allowed to have any material possessions or have a career which generates income.

St. Augustine later on pursued dropped Manichaeism and pursue priesthood where his written works influenced both Roman Catholics and other Christians. He became the bishop of Hippo, hence the name, "St. Augustine of Hippo".

Doctrine of the Original Sin

We are all aware of the story of Adam and Eve in the book of Genesis in the Bible. In this story, Eve was tricked the serpent to pick a forbidden fruit from the tree of life. Eve shared it with Adam, who also took a bite from the fruit, instead of rebuking her.

The serpent turned out to be Satan, luring them into committing the first and original sin. This caused to be thrown out of Eden and this is said to be the start of a harsh life, where women had to suffer childbirth pains, where man would grow old and die, and thorns grew out of plants and flowers.

Being the original sinners, St. Augustine believed, we inherited the sins of Adam and Eve, and the only way for us to be free of this mortal sin is through salvation, sealed by the sacrament of baptism. Moreover, he believed that "lust" is an independent feeling and a manifestation of the original sin. Lust is a hindrance to having a virtuous life and must be cast out of a person's mind.

Remarkable Works: *"Confessions", "City of God", "On Christian Doctrine", and "Handbook on Faith, Hope, and Love"*

- Thomas Aquinas (1225 – 1274)
  Nationality: Italian
  Title: *"Father of Thomism"*
  Famous Line: *"Friendship is source of the greatest pleasures, and without friends even the most agreeable pursuits become tedious."*

  "Good can exist without evil, whereas evil cannot exist without good."

  "To live well is to work well, to show a good activity."

Known for: "Quinquae Viae" (Five Proofs of the Existence of God)

Thomas Aquinas is known for bridging the gap between religion and reason, proving the existence of God with reasoning and his "five proofs" (the five proofs of the existence of God), thus making a huge impact on Christian beliefs.

With this, he bridged the gap between science and religion, which have contradicted each other for as long as we remember. He was also called "Thomas of Aquin" or "Thomas of Aquino". Thomas Aquinas was known as a Christian theologian, but at the same time, he was a philosopher, an empiricists and Aristotleian, to be specific.

For him, faith and reason should not be viewed as contradictory but "supplementary. To explain this, truth and knowledge have two types:

- **Natural Revelation**

    This is the truth gained from correct human reasoning.

- **Supernatural Revelation or Divine Intervention**

    In this, truth is faith-based and upholds the teachings of God's scripture as true as written in the Holy Bible.

    Arguments on the validity of the Bible have always been a hot issue for philosophers then and now. Since for Christians, the Bible is the Word of God, skeptics argue whether God is real or not. They disprove the existence and truth in both God and the Bible because its contents were collectively written by different people from different time periods and walks of life.

    Why should the Bible be an evidence of divinity and a supernatural presence if it was only written by people as well, just like any other books and articles?

    Thomas Aquinas answered this question by using the idea of "supernatural revelation". Although the Bible was written by different hands, they were under divine intervention, meaning God was dictating them what to right.

As evidence, every book of the Bible, though written in different time periods are always in line with each other and the information written in it were also proven to be historically relevant. A mere human couldn't have written such an elaborate book, if it wasn't for a supernatural revelation.

Thomas Aquinas believed that faith and reason should work together and not against each other in achieving truth and knowledge. Faith and reason are supplementary and not contradictory.

"Quinquae Viae"

In this book, Thomas Aquinas justified the existence of God citing five proofs.

1. **Ex Motu (Argument of the Unmoved Mover)** – everything is in moving, the Earth itself is moving; no matter how far reasoning goes, there would be no explanation as to who or what is the mover of all movers, which is the source of all that is moving, and thus, cannot be moved anymore. God is the mover who controls all other motions.

2. **Ex Causa (Argument of the First Cause)** – the cause of somethings have always been the reason of studies and questions; these causes would then have preceding causes, so on and so forth, so there has to be a first cause of everything, there is and being the first cause, it cannot be uncaused anymore. God is the first cause.

3. **Ex Contingentia (Argument from Contingency)** – one thing comes from something. Something can't come from nothing, or else it wouldn't have existed in the first place. The first thing has to come from something. God's existence is not contingent. He is the necessary Being that is not dependent on anything rather from whom everything depends upon.

4. **Ex Gradu (Argument from Degree or Gradation)** – goodness have varying degrees; one's level of goodness may be higher than that of the other. To whom or what do we compare the perfection of this gradation? There has to be and Absolute Good Being from which the levels are compared to.

5. **Ex Fine (Argument from Design)** – also called the "teleological argument; everything is by design, from the lower forms to the highest form of life, which is man. God is the intelligent designer behind all of these.

Remarkable Works: *"Summa Theologica" (Compendium of Theology), "Summa Contra Gentiles" "On the Truth of the Catholic Faith), and "quinquae viae" (Five Ways)*

- John Wycliffe (1320 – 1384)
  Nationality: English
  Title: The evening star of scholasticism , the morning star of the English Reformation.
  Famous Line: *"I believe that in the end the truth will conquer."*

  > *"Visit those who are sick, or who are in trouble, especially those whom God has made needy by age, or by sickness, as the feeble, the blind, and the lame who are in poverty. These you shall relieve with your goods after your power and after their need, for thus biddeth the Gospel."*

  > *"The higher the hill, the stronger the wind: so the loftier the life, the stronger the enemy's temptations."*

  Known for: Wycliffe's Bible
  Remarkable Works: The Complete Wycliffe Bible: Old Testament, New Testament & Apocrypha, Trialogus

- John Huss (1369 – 1415)
  Nationality: Czechoslovakian
  Title: Inspirer of Hussitism
  Famous Line: *"He that fears death loses the joy of life."*

"It is better to die than to live badly."

"Seek the truth, listen to the truth, teach the truth, love the truth, abide by the truth, and defend the truth unto death."

Known for: Theology
Remarkable Works: *An important predecessor to Protestantism and a seminal figure in the Bohemian Reformation.*

- Desiderius Erasmus (1466 – 1536)
  Nationality: Dutch
  Title: Prince of the Humanists
  Famous Line: *"Give light, and the darkness will disappear of itself."*

  "When I get a little money, I buy books; and if any is left, I buy food and clothes."

  "Prevention is better than cure."

  Known for: Criticism of Protestantism, Renaissance humanism, Christian Philosophy.
  Remarkable Works: *"In Praise of folly"*, *"On Civility of children"*, *"Handbook of a Christian Knight"*.

- Niccolo Machiavelli (1469 – 1527)
  Nationality: Italian
  Title: *"Father of Machiavellianism"*
  Famous Line: *"The end justifies the means."*

  "Whosoever desire constant success must change his conduct with the times."

  "It is not the titles that honor men, but men that honor the titles."

  Known for: Machiavellianism

Aside from his famous line, The end justifies the means", Niccolo Machiavelli is also popular for another line which was, "It is far better to be feared than love."

"Machiavellianism" centered on a philosophy which advocated rulers to govern their territories with ruthlessness, authority, order, and control, instead of love and compassion as his contradictors emphasized.

Remarkable Works: *"The Prince", "The Art of War"*

- Michel de Montaigne (1533 – 1592)
Nationality: French
Title: "The French Seneca"
Famous Line: *"Lend yourself to others, but yourself to yourself."*

"There is no conversation more boring than the one where everybody agrees."

"The world is but a perpetual see-saw."

Known for: Popularizing the essay as a literary genre.
Remarkable Works: *"The Complete Essays"*

- Thomas Hobbes (1588 – 1679)
Nationality: English
Title: Thomas Hobbes of Malmesbury
Famous Line: *"Scientia potentia est. (Knowledge is power)"*
"A man's conscience and his judgment is the same thing; and as the judgment, so also the conscience, may be erroneous."

"The source of every crime is some defect of the understanding; or some error in reasoning; or some sudden force of the passions."

Known for: Political Philosophy
Remarkable Works: *"Leviathan"*

- René Descartes (1596 – 1650)
Nationality: French

Title: Father of Modern Philosophy
Famous Line: *"Cogito, ergo sum." ("I think, therefore I am.")*

> *"It is not enough to have a good mind; the main thing is to use it well."*

> *"Each problem that solved became a rule, which served afterwards, to solve other problems."*

Known for: Cartesian Dualism

René Descartes believed in the separation of mind and matter or mind and body. He believed that your body is a physical thing but your mind and your thoughts are non-physical.

Your mind and your body, although separate, interact with each other. Therefore, your non-physical mind dictates what your physical body would say and do.

You can say one thing is real not because you can physically see and touch it, but because your mind believes it is real.

Remarkable Works: *"Discours de la Methode (Discourse on the Method)"* , *"The Meditations"*, and *"Les Passions de l'âme (The passions of the soul)"*

- John Locke (1632 – 1704)
  Nationality: English
  Title: Father of Liberalism
  Famous Line: *"All mankind, being all equal and independent, no one ought to harm another in his life, health, liberty, or possession."*

  > *"To love our neighbor as ourselves is such a truth for regulating human society, that by that alone, one might determine all the cases in social morality."*

  > *"All wealth is the product of labor."*

  Known for: Theory of Blank Slate

In John Locke's "Blank Slate Theory", all of us were born with a mind that was as clear as blank slate, no thoughts, no ideas, and definitely no reasoning yet. But as we grew older, we perceived more and more. Therefore what we are today, is dictated by our past. Meaning to say, your attitude, behavior, beliefs, opinion, and way of thinking, came to be as a product of all your life experiences summed up. Your experiences shaped you into who you are now.

Remarkable Works: "An Essay Concerning Human Understanding", "Two Treatises of Government", "A Letter Concerning Toleration"

- George Berkeley (1685 – 1753)
  Nationality: Irish
  Title: Bishop Berkeley
  Famous Line: *"Truth is the cry of all, but the game of few."*

  "Few men think; yet all have opinions. "

  "I had rather be an oyster than a man, the most stupid and senseless of animals."

  Known for: Immaterialism
  Remarkable Works: *"An essay Towards A New Theory of Vision"*, *"A Treatise Concerning the Principles of Human Knowledge"*

- David Hume (1711–1776)
  Nationality: Scottish
  Title: "Le Bon David" (The Good David)
  Famous Line: *"A wise man proportions his belief to the evidence."*

  "Be a philosopher but, amid all your philosophy, be a man."

  "It's when we start working together that the real healing takes place. It's when we start spilling our sweat, and not our blood."

  Known for: Feelings over Reason

  David Hume lived in the so-called, **"age of reasoning"**, wherein a person is normally judged according to how good he is with rationality and use it to either prove or disprove an idea or opinion.

But David Hume believed that the mind is not the only thing that must be trained. He believed that our feelings, or "passions" as he called it, should also be trained. He argued that what we choose to do is driven by our passions, or what we feel like doing. What we decide do to is not only dictated by our mind but also by our feelings.

In doing so, people should be educated on how to feel, to be patient, kind, considerate, benevolent, while pursuing their passions.

David Hume also suggested that the educational system should also address feelings, not just reason and university professors should teach not as philosophers, but as people with sympathy, encouragement, creativity, and good example, hence his famous line, "Be a philosopher, but amidst all your philosophy, be still a man."

Remarkable Works: *"A Treatise of Human Nature", and "Philosophy by David Hume"*

- Jean-Jacques Rousseau (1712 – 1778)
  Nationality: Swiss
  Title:
  Famous Line: *"The world of reality has its limits; the world of imagination is boundless."*

  "What wisdom can you find that is greater than kindness?"

  "The strongest is never strong enough to be always the master, unless he transforms strength into right, and obedience into duty."

  Known for: "General Will" "Amour de Soi" "Simplicity of Humanity"
  Remarkable Works: *"Discourse on Inequality" "The Social Contract"*

- Immanuel Kant (1724 – 1804)

Nationality: German
Title:
Famous Line: *"Happiness is not an ideal of reason but of imagination."*

"Dare to know! Have the courage to use your own intelligence."

"Science is organized knowledge. Wisdom is organized life."

Known for: Moral Law

Immanuel Kant believed that, although people differ with what they believe in, there is a standard "Moral Law", which dictates "how things really are and ought to be", and our belief and actions should be directed by these moral laws.

Remarkable Works: *"Critique of Pure Reason (Kritik der reinen Vernunft)"*

- William Godwin (1756 – 1836)
  Nationality: English
  Title:
  Famous Line: *"He that loves reading has everything within his reach."*

  "The proper method for hastening the decay of error is by teaching every man to think for himself."

  "Study with desire is real activity; without desire it is but the semblance and mockery of activity."

  Known for: Anarchism
  Remarkable Works: *"Sketches of History", "New Annual Register", "Things As They Are"*

- George Wilhelm Friedrich Hegel (1770 – 1831)
  Nationality: German
  Title:
  Famous Line: *"We learn from history that we do not learn from history."*

> *"Genuine tragedies in the world are not conflicts between right and wrong. They are conflicts between two rights."*

> *"Education is the art of making man ethical."*

Known for: "Absolute Idealism" "Hegelian Dialectics" "Alienation"
Remarkable Works: *"The Phenomenology of Spirit"*, *"Science of Logic"*

- John Stuart Mill (1806 – 1873)
  Nationality: English
  Title:
  Famous Line: *"I have learned to seek my happiness by limiting my desires, rather than in attempting to satisfy them."*

  > *"Bad men need nothing more to compass their ends, than that good men should look on and do nothing."*

  > *"If all mankind minus one were of one opinion, mankind would be no more justified in silencing that one person than he, if he had the power, would be justified in silencing mankind."*

  Known for: Utilitarianism, Classical Liberalism
  Remarkable Works: *"On Liberty"*, and *"System of Logic"*

- Karl Marx (1818 – 1883)
  Nationality: German
  Title: *"Father of Marxism"*
  Famous Line: *"The philosophers have only interpreted the world, in various ways. The point, however, is to change it."*

  > *"History calls those men the greatest who have ennobled themselves by working for the common good; experience acclaims as happiest the man who has made the greatest number of people happy."*

  > *"Reason has always existed, but not always in a reasonable form."*

Known for: Marxism

The ideas and publications of Karl Marx has laid foundations for today's communism and socialism. In his philosophy called **"Marxism",** he addressed the various issues which surround the existing class systems where nations and communities are divided into classes, based on their social status.

He argued that these class systems created a huge gap between the rich and the poor and was more advantageous for the rich. Thus, the rich became even richer, and the poor became even poorer. Moreover, the poor (lower classes) were ruled over by the rich (upper classes).

Remarkable Works: *"Das Kapital (Capital)", and "The Communist Manifesto"*

- Burrhus Frederic Skinner (B.F.Skinner) (1904 – 1990)
  Nationality: American
  Title:
  Famous Line: *"A failure is not always a mistake. It may simply, be the best one can do."*

  "The major difference between rats and people is that rats learn from experience."

  "We shouldn't teach good books, we should teach a love of reading. Knowing the contents of a few works of literature is a trivial achievement. Being inclined to go on reading is a great achievement."

Known for: Operation Conditioning, Radical Behaviorism, Verbal Behavior, Behavior Analysis.
Remarkable Works: *"Schedules of Reinforcement"*

C. Eastern Philosophers

Lao Tzu or Laozi (600 BC)
Nationality: Chinese
Title: *"Founder of Taoism or Daoism", "Old Teacher"*
Famous Line: *"If you are depressed you are living in the past, if you are anxious you are living in the future. If you are at peace, you are living in the present."*

"When you are content to be simply yourself and don't compare or compete, everybody will respect you."

"Great acts are made up of small deeds."

Known for: Taoism or Daoism

Taoism is a native religion and philosophy in China as well as Confucianism and was founded by Lao Tzu, also called Laozi or Lao Tze. This is not his real name, rather a name which translates as "Old Teacher" or "Old Man". His given name was Li Er.

He was older than another well-known philosopher, Confucius, and sources say that they have crossed paths in the past, and therefore have lived in the same century. It can be accepted that Lao Tzu was a senior mentor for Confucius, although there were still differences in their philosophical teachings.

In Taoism, "Tao" means the "Way", or path in which all people should travel to. In this philosophy, Lao Tzu teaches that all human beings are naturally good but are corrupted by evil. Therefore, the bad actions we do are not caused entirely by us but also by the evil forces which influenced us to do so.

"Tao" is the natural order of the universe and the energy flowing in all that exists. One of the most popular teachings in Taoism is the concept of "yin and yang", the black and white swirls which, together, forms a circle.

Yin and yang signifies the balances of life and how opposites are not opponents or contradictors. Rather, for one to exist, it must work well with the other.

For Example: *12 hours of day and 12 hours of day*

Left and right hand used to carry heavy objects

Left eye and right to see in a wider view

Changes of seasons (winter, spring, summer, fall)

One cannot be right when no one is proven wrong; One can right his wrong by analyzing what makes the wrong, wrong, and then make it right.

There are days when we are completely happy and days when we shed tears

The color black looks good and stands out on a white background, vice versa.

The sun dries out the rain, the rain cools off the intense heat of the sun.

Following the concept of yin and yang in human relationship, it can be put that "you should not fight fire with fire. The conflicts which happen every single day is caused by people not realizing that peace is achieved by understanding the "Tao" or way of the other, and working with them instead of against them.

What normally happens is, we try to prove ourselves right and superior over others, and they would want to do the same to us. It's a never-ending cycle. But Lao Tzu taught the contrary.

Remarkable Work: *"Tao Te Ching (Book of the Way)"*

Confucius (551 BC - 479 BC)
   Nationality: Chinese
   Title: Founder of Confucianism
   Famous Line: *"Do not do unto others what you do not want others to do unto you."*

"If you hate a person, then you're defeated by them."

Known for: Filial Piety *(xiào)*

This cites the importance of your family and upholding family traditions. Filial piety is considered the most important Chinese moral philosophy which has been around for over 3,000 years.

Filial piety emphasizes that children must show their love, loyalty, respect, support, and deference to their parents and other elder family members and relatives like your grandparents and older brothers and sisters.

Your parent and elder relatives have tried their best to love you and provide for you, have sent you to school, showered you with gifts and luxuries, and cared for you every time you get sick.

Filial piety is acknowledging that with everything they have given you, children are forever indebted to their parents. But this is a debt of gratitude and is not taken negatively.

When everyone turns their backs on you, your family should be there to have your back.

How can you practice filial piety? It's simple. You can practice filial piety by simply:

- ✓ Obeying your parents and the rules they set inside the house.
- ✓ Not answering back or shouting at your parents, grandparents, and older siblings.
- ✓ Taking care of your parents and elder relatives when they get old and cannot take care of themselves.
- ✓ Obeying your parents' wishes.
- ✓ Providing for your family when are older and capable, just like what they did for you as you were growing up. This includes material needs, food, and money.
- ✓ Comforting the elderly when they have problems or are feeling down.

✓ Pampering them and remembering important events such as birthdays.
✓ Being with the family on important days such as birthdays, holidays, and Chinese festivals.

Jesus Christ also stated an active perspective of Confucius' philosophy, using the word "do" instead of "do not". It goes, "Do unto others as you would have them do to you" (Luke 6:31).

Remarkable Works: *"The Analects"*

Mohandas Karamchand Gandhi (Mahatma Gandhi)
Nationality: Indian
Title: *"Mahatma (The Great Soul)"*
Famous Line: *"The future depends on what we do in the present."*

"In a gentle way, you can shake the world."

"If we are to teach real peace in this world, and if we are to carry on a real war against war, we shall have to begin with the children."

Known for: "Satyagraha" (Truth and Firmness)

Mahatma Gandhi was an Indian philosopher, lawyer, and activist who led the nationalist movement of the Indian people against the British colonizers. He is considered to be the "Father of Independence" as he was one of the primary leaders of the independence movement in India.

He is famous for the "Satyagraha", a peaceful protest against the brutality carried out by the British colonizers, which sparked a sort of mass civil disobedience among the people, crying out for reforms. Satyagraha simply aimed to advocate human rights and social justice for the Indians under British rule.

He walked with a huge number of protesters holding in his hands not a rifle or a sword, but a walking stick. Mahatma Gandhi believed in a non-violent protest called "civil resistance", and through this, he taught the world not to fight fire with fire, in order to achieve independence and social change for India.

Despite advocating a peaceful protest, Mahatma Gandhi had six assassination attempts. He made a huge impact not only in India but across the world. Unfortunately, he was killed by Nathuram Godse, a Hindu fanatic who did not agree with Gandhi's efforts of promoting a peaceful harmony between Hindus and Muslims.

Gandhi's Satyagraha teaches us to practice the non-violence of the mind to uphold the spirit of peace and love in humanity, to create harmony among people regardless of their racial and religious differences.

Remarkable Wo: *"India of My Dreams", and "The Story of my Experiments with Truth (Mahatma Gandhi's Autobiography)"*

Siddhartha Gautama (Buddha)
Nationality: Indian

Title: *"The Enlightened God", "Founder of Buddhism"*

Famous Line: *"The mind is everything. What you think you become. What you feel, you attract. What you imagine, you create."*

"Teach this triple truth to all: A generous heart, kind speech, and a life of service and compassion are the things which renew humanity."

"The tongue like a sharp knife - kills without drawing blood."

Known for: Buddhism

Buddhism is considered as the oldest religion in history which taught ancient knowledge and wisdom still applied by many in the modern period. It is so old that no one for sure knows how exactly old it is. It's literally as old as people could remember.

It was founded by Siddhartha Gautama more commonly known as Buddha. Although we imagine Buddha as fat because of how he is portrayed in some figurines, Buddha was actually slim, because his teaching would be contrary to obesity

You might not know of this, but before he became who he was, he was actually a prince. He searched for his own truth and lived in isolation until he found the ultimate wisdom under a Bodhi tree, and thus became Buddha, translated as "The Enlightened One".

Buddha's teaching laid the foundations of Buddhism as both a religion and a philosophy. Below are some of the key teachings or philosophies of Buddhism.

Reincarnation

This is the process of rebirth and a cause-and-effect chain as a consequence to the life we've lived. This means that good deeds come with good consequences as much as bad deeds come with bad consequences.

In reincarnation, a person undergoes a process of continuous rebirth until he reaches "nirvana" or "enlightenment".

As you undergo reincarnation you can be reborn into any kind of livings things, depending on how you've lived your previous life. You can be a cat, dog, even lice in your next life. If you've lived a good life, you might be reincarnated as a higher form of life.

There was a story about a foreigner who visited India. He rode a taxi and noticed that the driver has lice on his shoulders. He politely called the attention of the driver. But instead of squishing the lice dead, he gently picked it up and put it back on his hair saying that they don't kill even a small head lice, as this might be a relative which has been reborn as a lice.

But no one knows if this is true because someone has to die first to find out and then come back again with the memory of his past life. This is not the case in Buddhism, because when you are reborn, you come back as a blank slate.

What would you be in your next life if you become reincarnated? Have you given it a thought?

The Truth About Suffering

The truth about our suffering is in Buddha's doctrine called, the "Four Noble Truths" which teaches the following:

Suffering, pain, and misery exist in life.

Suffering or "dukkha" is part of living. The world is far from perfect and no one on Earth is promised with a life free of suffering. We all experience heartache, sickness, failure, pain, aging, tiredness, depression, and eventually death. No person is exempted from all these sufferings.

Suffering arises from attachment to desires.

According to Buddha, suffering is caused by having desires which were unmet. Some of these desires aren't even necessary to go on living.

For example, Buddha is not fat because he eats only what his body requires to stay nourished and active. He teaches contrary to gluttony and was actually slim. Food is a necessity but people sometimes crave to eat more than what they need.

When you don't manage to consume the food you desire, suffering happens, especially when you start comparing what you eat with what others eat. Why can't we eat at KFC today like my friends?

Another example is owning a mobile phone. Even if you already have a functional one, you still eye for the latest in iPhone or Samsung, because everyone else you know does. When your parents can't afford to purchase one for you, you start feeling down, thinking that other people's lives are better than yours just because they can keep up with the trend.

Buddha teaches that in order to live a fulfilling life, you need to free yourself from your desires, thus freeing yourself from suffering.

Suffering ceases when attachment to desire ceases.

From the examples states in the second noble truth, you can cause your own suffering but go on blaming other people for it.

If you let go of your desires, especially those which are unnecessary and prioritize living according to your means. You can be free of suffering. Nirvana is simply the freedom from all your worries and troubles in life.

Freedom from suffering is possible by practicing the Eightfold Path.

The Eightfold Path is a list of eight paths or attitude a person needs in order to free himself from suffering, enumerated below.

Right view
Right intention
Right speech

Right action
Right livelihood
Right effort
Right mindfulness
Right concentration

Remarks: *Buddha had nothing written down but his words were orally past down generation by generation. The best scripture claiming to be Buddha's utterances is the "Buddhavacana" or "Words of Buddha", which was written hundreds of years after his death.*

Chapter 5 – Answers to the Questions You Ask Yourself

Metaphysics

What is Reality

Reality is the entirety of all that exists within a particular system, in other words, it is the sum of all that appears to be real in that system, as opposed to thing's that are virtual or imaginary. Reality also refers to the existential status of things, revealing their existence. With regards to physical terms, reality is the entirety of the components of a system, both the known components and the unknown components.

Reality has different categories, it could be Constructed, Objective, Subjective, Empirical, Instrumental, and other realities. Whichever category one intends to look at, the bottom-line will always be that reality is an idea that is backed up by confidence, an acceptable collective representation of how things are.

Constructed Reality

Constructed reality, better known as Social Construction of Reality, refers to the theory that the manner in which we present ourselves to other people is molded partially by our interactions with them, and also by the experiences we've had. How we were brought up, conditions around our upbringing, things we were raised to believe, how we were raised to see and handle situations, all these have an influence on how we present ourselves to other people, how we feel about ourselves and how we feel about other people too.

In essence, our background and beliefs influence our perception of reality. Furthermore, our reality is somewhat an entangled negotiation. What we identify as real depends on what is socially and collectively acceptable, while we partake in the construction of reality, it's not entirely a product of our actions.

Take for example the case of a wealthy individual and a low-income earner. Bob is a wealthy individual whose needs have been satisfied many times over, buys his pet dog an organic food that costs more than the weekly earnings of the low-income earner. Bob feels satisfied, proud and happy that he is capable of taking good care of his pet dog and is adamant that it is the appropriate thing to do if one really cherishes his pet dog, after all, it was the veterinary doctor who recommended such diet. Bob who offloads food from the wealthy individual's car might be annoyed or saddened when he gets to know how much the wealthy individual spends on his pet dog, he might even be more pissed off when he realizes that the wealthy individual's pet eats better than he does, and starts to wonder if the wealthy man has any idea of reality, the reality which he (the low-income earner), has been made to know.

How we see and handle everyday issues depends on our experiences and respective backgrounds. By interacting with others, the wealthy individual has learnt that, taking care of one's pet, regardless of the expenses, is a worthy thing to do. Meanwhile, the low-income earner, based on what he's even experiencing, sees spending on a pet a detrimental thing to do. So clearly, both of them have different perceptions and approach to a particular situation.

Objective and Subjective Reality

Objective and subjective reality, better known as objectivity and subjectivity respectively. The difference between these two in philosophy is the judgement and claims that people make. Objective judgement and claims are inferred to be free from personal preferences and emotional attachments. Subjective judgement and claims on the other hand are said to be mostly influenced by such personal preferences.

For instance, when you make a statement such as "I am five feet tall", such a statement is considered to be objective because it is a precise measurement that is not influenced by personal likings and can be checked and examined by independent observers. However, statements such as "I like six feet tall guys" is subjective because it is entirely influenced by your personal preferences.

Empirical Reality

Empirical reality is based on empiricism, a theory that implies that knowledge and existence come only from primary experience. In other words, empiricism adopts empirical evidence in the formation of ideas and beliefs, rather than intuitive or inherited ideas or traditions. Empirical reality is the reality that can be authenticated with ample evidence that verifies it. As opposed to absolute reality, which is the utmost reality, that is not influenced by the beliefs or ideas of any finite being. Taking an instance from the environment, we can't see the atmosphere, but we believe is. But emperically, with the discovery of oxygen and nitrogen, and tests carried out shows that these two gases are present in the atmosphere, so that backs it up.

Plato's Idea of Reality

Platonic realism is the theory of reality that was brought forth by Plato. According to him, the obvious world of certain things is a changing exhibition, like the shadows displayed on the wall due to the activities carried out by their respective ideas and forms. Whereas, the world of certain things is virtual, they occupy a reality that can't be observed, yet these realities are true and certain.

Are Things We can't Touch Real?

Our sense of touch is the primary form of perceptual reality, though it has been replaced by our vision in most fields. The sense of touch cuts across the entire body parts via numerous receptors in the skin. Usually, it includes these signals with responses from the muscles and tendons as we go about actively, exploring our world, with proprioceptive impulses and deductions about our positions on surfaces. These attributes of touch raise quite a number of fascinating philosophical issues.

Are the things we can't touch real? We can answer this question by asking ourselves a few questions.

- You can't touch the hot weather, but is there truly hot weather?
- You can't touch the cold weather, but are you sure something called the cold weather exists?
- Ever tried touching the darkness at night? Do you think it's real?
- Have you tried to touch the light during the day? Does that imply that it's real?
- Those emotions, anger, happiness, depression, sadness etc. Do they exist?
- That force attracting and repulsing the two magnets you have in your hands, does it truly exist?

Have you answered those questions? Do things we can't touch the exist now? The obvious answer is our sense of touch isn't entirely a perception verification of existence for everything, it has limits. When it comes to abstract things, our sense of touch can't ascertain the reality of such situations. Hence, in cases like this, our sense of sight and the sensory receptors in our skin proves the existence of such things. This further promotes the theory of platonic realism that some things are certain, they occupy a true reality but are virtual.

Is this World Real or am I Dreaming?

The problem posed by the question, 'what is reality?' arises from a consciousness of ourselves as people who live in a world which appears to be outside of, and yet is the origin of, our conscious life. Our thoughts on this makes us wonder if we can have an idea of the world beyond our perceptions which is the fundamental cause of our consciousness of appearances. This world of the elementary is what is termed 'reality'.

Staring at a bottle of soda I'm holding, I reason that what I'm seeing isn't is not the bottle of soda as it exists out there, in the reality. Rather, what I am staring at is the image of the soda bottle produced in my brain with the aid of my sensory perceptions. In other words, my senses analyze the data about the object of my perception, in this case, a bottle of soda, and utilizing these sensory data my brain produces an image for me to see.

At any point, what I see is the picture brought up in my brain and not the bottle of soda in my hand. However, due to the fact that the image in my brain is not the object itself, one may question the existential nature of the object out there, that is, in reality. How then can we confirm whether the objects actually exist externally, if all that is exhibited to us is the image in our heads? Is this world actually real or it's just a world of ideas or dreams? The answer to this is, our world is both. Reality is somewhat a world of ideas and also an objective world of an empirical form of reality.

Even though one may not have perceptions of physical objects asides our perception of them, one could come to a final note that objects out there are actually there, and as such they're real, owing to the fact that there is a general agreement about them. If I throw the bottle of soda in my hand at a passer-by and it hits the person's head, he/she would report to the police that I threw a bottle of soda at him, as opposed to saying I hit him with the image of a soda bottle. Generally, we agree, as to what things are, if there were no consensus about the external world we perceive, then our experiences would be everything we're sure of.

Is time Real or an Illusion?

"Time is nature's way of keeping everything from happening at once," -Physics Nobel laureate Steven Wreinberg , University of Texas, Austin. To us, time is the transition of the sun and seasons, the irreversible wrinkling of our skin. Time is the legible indicator of a present that is progressing, and a future that is definitely becoming the past. We are born, we crawl, we stand, we walk, we grow, we age, we give birth, we get old, we die. These are some of the realities and events that happen in human life, the span between these events is what we call Time. Time is that entity that passes consistently irrespective of whatever happens in the world. It is an undeniable entity that orders our lives.

In the philosophy of time, it is crucial that we mention two concepts, which are Eternalism and Presentism. Eternalism, as a philosophical approach to the existential nature of time, holds that all existence in time (past, present and future) is equally really real. Eternalism makes an instance where it gives time an ontology of being a dimension with different times occurring as real different places, therefore future events have already occurred there, in essence, there is no objective transition of time. Whereas presentism, otherwise known as the growing block universe theory of time, holds that the future isn't similar to any other time.

The concept that time is independently non-existent is also quite relevant. Some philosophers and researchers believe that the existence of time only depends on the mind. Henri Bergson, a renowned French philosopher, mentioned that real time, which he referred to as duration, only exists in our consciousness. What Henri meant was that time is merely a concept that exists in our mind, we have grown to get used to it. The duration from which we grow from babies to teenagers is time, the period between us being teenagers and parents is time. Time isn't restricted to what you see on the wall clock or in that fancy Ben10 wrist watch you're putting on, we live through time.

Which is the Person, the Body or the Mind?

In philosophy, there's a phenomenon called The mind-body problem. The mind-body problem is a core issue in the philosophy of mind. Two essential schools of thought attributed to the mind-body problem are Dualism and Monism. In the philosophy of mind, dualism is a theory that claims that the mind and the body, that is the mental and physical, are in certain things instances, different entities. Dualism was propounded in the 17th century by **Rene Descartes**, a western philosopher. Under dualism, there are categories, Substance Dualism and Property Dualism. Substance dualists are of the motion that mind exists on its own as a substance, while property dualists are maintaining a stance that the mind is a group of separate entities that emanate from, but not limited to, the brain.

Monism on the other hand states that the mind and the body are not existentially separate entities, but are, however, not dependent. This was first brought forth by **Parmenides** in the 5th Century BCE.

A person is composed of both the physical and mental aspects. We have certain attributes that are related to physical sciences, such physical properties as weight, shape, size, color etc. As stated earlier, the mental properties we possess are not attributed to the common physical objects, these properties include consciousness, including perceptual experience, emotional experience, and many other forms, intentionality (including beliefs, desires, and much else), they are attributed to an object or a self.

If the mind and body are separate entities, in the way that they are needed by either substance dualism or property dualism, then one begins to wonder how they are related. Layman's knowledge will tell us that these two entities actually interact with each other, come to think of it, our thoughts and feelings most of the time are triggered by bodily events. In like manner, our thoughts and feelings give rise to bodily responses. This tells us that they influence each other. For example, most of the time, it is the thought of eating a particular food or snack that makes you stand up from bed and go straight to the kitchen to prepare that food. Also, if a knife is aimed at you, the thought of being injured or dying is what makes get out of that path as quickly as you can, these are instances of your thoughts controlling your bodily responses.

Different philosophers have different opinions when it comes to the mind-body problem. However, **John Locke**, a modern philosopher believes that the mind is the real person, and the body is only a possession. He stated that if the mind is removed from a person, the body is only a material reality. For him, the mind is the real person, and in the real body, the body section is integrated perfectly into it, and in every person, the mind controls the body even though they influence each other.

What is the Meaning of Life?

The meaning of life concerns the general significance of living and existence. Providing an answer to this question would require you to ask yourself a few related questions such as "What is life all about?", "What is the purpose of existence?" "Why are we here?". There have been many proposed answers to these questions emanating from different ideological perspectives. What is the meaning of life? , breaking this question down, what do we mean by the meaning of life? Are we referring to human life in general or the meaning of life of each specific individual living it? Based on the context, "meaning" in the question, "What is the meaning of life?" can be said to mean "purpose." It could also be said to mean intention or significance.

Life is attached to the state of being conscious existence, in other words, being alive. Understanding the importance of life is somewhat complicated, not only because of broad interpretation range of "Meaning," but also, we do not know what the word " Life" implies in this context. Questions on Life generally span across the following instances:

1- Life = the life of each person, that is, my life and your life. The life of each individual being is what separates people who are alive from those that are dead.

2-Life= the entire humanity. This implies the existence of humanity.

3- Life= the totality of biological life. This covers all living organisms in general.

4- Life= all of space-time existence.

5- Life= an unpleasant marker of those stages in human life that are attributed with a kind of existential austerity, serious concerns, and prone to extreme questioning by human beings.

Understand each of these options helps us to provide appropriate interpretation and answers to the question.

What seems undeniable is the fact that life has no other meaning except the meaning we've acquired by our consciousness, passed on to us through our genes, gotten from experiences, or the content given to us via culture, ideology, background, environment, beliefs. Hence, the meaning of life that we're supposed to have, vary ideologically, culturally, and individually. However, the range of these meanings may be from straightforward and easy meanings to highly complex meanings. For instance, to some people, the meaning of life to most fathers could be being able to cater for the needs of the family, for Tom, what life meant to him was capturing Jerry, for Peter Parker A.K.A Spiderman, what life meant to him was being able to spin those webs, the moment he lost that ability, he became miserable, for others it could be through painting, singing, uncovering the truth through philosophy, and so on. A common attribute of these examples is that they all involve a consciousness that is positively(or negatively) and effectively absorbed, committed, engaged, delighted, improved, and fulfilled.

Furthermore, the meaning of life to each individual may dwindle over time due to decline, unpleasant or tragic occurrences. Sadly, at this stage, it might be hard even to see what life is or attach any significant meaning to life. Likewise, the meaning of life to each and every one of us might change as we move from a phase of life to another due to maturity, new interests, personal development, or commitments. The meaning of life, therefore, varies for each person due to vast majority of reasons; however, it boils down to what makes one happy and fulfilled.

What is Free will?

In humans, free will is the enablement or ability to pick among options or to act in specific circumstances independent of regular, social, or divine limitations. The concept of free will is hindered by certain proponents claiming determinism. Contentions for free will depend on the abstract understanding of freedom, on opinion of guilt, on uncovered religion, and on the general notion of responsibility regarding individual activities that underlie the ideas of law, rewards, punishment and incentives. In philosophy, determinism is a theory that claims that all events and happenings, including moral decisions, are controlled by previously existing causes. Determinism is typically believed to oppose free will because it is of the opinion that people can't act in any case than they do.

The theory holds that the universe is absolutely discerning because that entire knowledge on some random situations guarantees that accurate information on its future is likewise possible. Minimally, to state that a person has free will is to believe that the person has the ability to determine his/her course of action. Be that as it may, even animals seem to fulfill this free will concept, and we usually believe that only human beings, and not animals, are entitled to free will. At this point, we can understand that free will as unique enablement to people that permits them to control their actions.

The primary reason the concept of free will is of utmost importance is that it is closely related to two other significant philosophical issues which are freedom of action and moral responsibilities. We generally have a common belief that a person's free actions are those activities that she does by virtue of exercising her free will. Take, for instance, a lady, Ella, who is thinking seriously about an essential free action, for example, whether to walk her pet dog or not. Ella may reason within herself, "I'm aware that I should take the dog for a while, it's been a while since she exercised, but in like manner, I would prefer not to take her for a walk since it is cold outside. However, I think, generally speaking, the best choice to make is to take her for a stroll."

Thus, we notice that one cogent reason why free will is important is because it appears to be necessary to carry out free action— Ella has first to decide to walk the pet dog before she takes her outside for the walk. Perhaps we assume that human actions are those activities that are the outcome of rational capacities of human, we, at that point, see that the chance of free activity relies upon the chance of unrestrained choice or free will: to claim that an individual acted uninhibitedly is to state that such individual successfully carried out that action of his/her choice. However, a significant portion of people thinks that the importance of free will doesn't stop at its necessity for free action and moral responsibility. Certain philosophers propose that free will is likewise a necessity for agency, sanity, the self-governance and dignity of people, innovativeness, participation, and the value of friendship and love.

Is God Real?

The existence of God has always been a subject of debate, mainly in the philosophy of religion and popular culture. A significant portion of the discussion about the existence of God can be grouped into metaphysical, logical, empirical, scientific, or subjective. However, in the philosophical aspect, questions pertaining to the existence of God cut across certain philosophical disciplines, which are:

- Epistemology: which talks about the nature and scope of knowledge.

- Ontology: which tells us about the nature of being, reality and existence.

- Theory of Value: since it's attributed to perfection.

Theism is the view and belief in the existence of a God, who is the creator, sustainer, and sustainer of the universe and he's unlimited when it comes to knowledge which means omniscient, powerful which means omnipotent, existent or present in all places and at all times which implies omnipresent, and moral perfection. The notion of God in philosophy is laced with the idea of God in religion. This is generally evident in figures like Augustine and Aquinas, who intended to bring more exactness and consistency to concepts discovered in religion. Others, similar to Leibniz and Hegel, interacted productively and profoundly with strict ideas. Indeed, even philosophers like Hume and Nietzsche, who condemned the idea of God, had to deal with the religious notions about God.

On the other hand, Western philosophy has most clearly meshed with Christianity, Judaism and Islam have had some impact. The orthodox forms of every one of the three religions have accepted the belief in a higher power (Theism), however, every religion has likewise yielded a wide range of different perspectives. Philosophy has demonstrated a similar variety, for instance, with regards to the starting cause for the world, Plato and Aristotle acknowledged God to be the crafter of uncreated matter. Plotinus viewed matter as emerging from God. Spinoza, departing from his

Judaistic origin, held God to be equivalent to the universe, while Hegel had a similar perspective by illustrating Christianity.

Issues identified with Western concepts of God include the nature of divine characteristics and how they can be known, whether that information can be conveyed or not, and how it can be conveyed, the idea of heavenly causality, and the connection between the divine and the human will.

The reality of God, in religion, is the proposition that there is a preeminent, supreme, heavenly or supernatural being that is the maker or sustainer and ruler of the universe and everything in it, including human beings. In numerous religions, God is likewise conceived as great, perfect and unfathomable by people, as almighty and all-knowing (omnipotent and omniscient), and as the origin and ultimate reason for morality. Mostly in its history, most religions have explicitly been interested about the topic of whether the existence of God can be proved rationally (i.e., either by virtue of reasoning alone or by reason influenced by personal or sense experience) or by an experience gained from religion, revelation or rather we should just accept it as a matter of faith.

The argument supporting the reality of God are generally grouped as either prior (from the earlier) or a posteriori—that is, based on an earlier of God or based on experience. An instance of the latter is the cosmological argument, which bids to the concept of causation to conclude either that there is an initial cause or that there is supreme being from whom every single being derive their existence. A different version of this methodology includes the appeal to possibility—to the fact that whatever is said to exist probably won't have existed and therefore calls for clarification, and the appeal to the principle of adequate reason, which guarantees that for anything that exists there must be a sufficient reason behind its existence.

The arguments by St. Thomas Aquinas known as the Five Ways—the argument from movement, from proficient causation, from possibility, from degrees of perfection, and conclusive causes or ends in nature—are generally viewed as cosmological. Something must be the first or prime mover, the principal efficient cause, the essential ground of creatures, the incomparable perfection that imperfect creatures emerge, and the shrewd guide of natural things toward their ends. This, Aquinas stated, is God.

The debate from the incipient likewise begins from human experience, in this situation, the perception of due process and reason in the natural world. The argument asserts that the universe is strongly comparable to, in its order and normality, an antique, for example, a watch; in light of the fact that the presence of the watch promotes the existence of a watchmaker, the presence of the universe backs up the reality of a divine creator of the universe, God.

Perhaps the most complex argument for the presence of God is the ontological or existential argument propounded by St. Anselm of Canterbury. According to Anselm, the notion of God as the absolutely perfect being—a being more prominent than which none can be considered— ascertains that God exists, because a being who is believed to be all perfect and fails to exist would be less great compared to a being who is all perfect and who exists

Perhaps the conditions of proof are too strict, and maybe there are several other ways to establish God's reality. Most prominent among these is the appeal to religious experience—an individual, direct associate with God, or an experience of God mediated through a religious convention. The Abrahamic religions (Judaism, Christianity, and Islam) likewise appeal to the concept of revelation, or to claims that God has spoken through selected messengers to unveil matters which would somehow or another be inaccessible. In Christianity, these issues have incorporated the idea of creation, the Trinity, and the Incarnation of Jesus Christ. Several endeavors have been made to set up the reasonableness of the concept of revelation through the witness of the church and through signs and supernatural occurrences(miracles), which are all thought to proclaim the genuine voice of God.

If God is Real, Why do Bad Things Happen?

In the philosophy of evil, theodicy implies vindication of God. It addresses the questions of why a good God allows the occurrence of evil, and it, therefore, addresses the issue of the problem of evil. Certain theodicies likewise address the evidential problem of evil by endeavoring to make the presence of an infinitely knowledgeable, all-mighty, and all-good God consistent with the presence of evil or suffering in the world.

The presence of evil and suffering in our reality tends to pose a serious challenge to the belief in the reality of a perfect and good God. We often think that if God is all-knowing, then he would already know all the bad things that happen in this world and even the horrible ones that are to happen. If God is almighty, He would be able to put an end to all the pains and suffering in the world. Besides, if God is morally perfect as stated, then definitely God would do something about all the bad things happening to innocent people, especially. Rather, we discover that our world is loaded up with incalculable cases of evil and bad situations. These statements about evil and suffering appear to oppose the claims of the orthodox theists that there exists an entirely good God.

The problem of evil is an exemplary difficulty in the philosophy of religion. The relative straightforwardness with which the issue can be expressed gives a false representation of the depth of the challenge that it presents to customary monotheism. Generally, it very well may be summed up as follows:

If God is omnipotent, it implies that He has the power to create a world devoid of evil.

If God is omniscient, that tells us that no evil occurrence goes divinely unnoticed.

If God is omnibenevolent, that points out that He has the intention of purging evil out of this world.

In this manner, the world ought to be perfect or at least be devoid of undeserved suffering. However, a glance reveals a world that unmistakably isn't free from unmerited suffering. Almost every day we hear disheartening stories; an earthquake killing hundreds of people, a pancreatic cancer patient suffers prolonged, excruciating pain and dies, a wild animal attacks a two-year-old child, angrily ripping his flesh and killing him, countless multitudes suffering in the ravages of war, Millions starving and dying due to famine, and other numerous terrible things of all kinds that happen in our world.

Therefore, the problem of evil poses the question, "How can a perfect divinity permit Injustice and uncontrolled evil in the world he created?

Numerous solutions to the problem of evil (theodicies) have been proposed. There is the debate of free will, ascribing evil not to God, but humankind's abuse of its freedom. Several are of the opinion that specific kinds of moral goodness – sympathy, for example – are not possible in a world without evil, and the estimation of these kinds of goodness exceeds the evils on which their existence depends. There is additionally what is termed 'the big picture defense', claiming that evil just shows up the way it is from our limited viewpoints. Had it been that we're able to see things from the point of view of God, we would see that all in all, every obvious evil assumes a fundamental role in making the world more perfect.

What is a Soul?

Soul, in religion and philosophy, is the immaterial aspect of a human being, the soul is that which confers individuality and humanity to us. The human soul is often considered to be synonymous with the mind. In theology, the soul is further explained as that part of a man that partakes of divinity and often is considered to survive the death of the body. Throughout history, the belief in the existence of a soul has been a common feature in most of the world's religions and cultures, nevertheless, some major religions oppose the concept of an eternal soul. Additionally, certain cultures are of the assertion the there's more than one soul in each person. The metaphysical concept of a soul is often associated with the concepts of reincarnation, heaven, and hell.

Additionally, various cultures have adopted some eternal principles of human life or existence correlative to the soul, and many have attributed souls to all living things. There is evidence even among people of ancient belief in an aspect distinct from the body, but this aspect resides in it. Despite popular and long-time belief in the existence of a soul, different religions and philosophers have developed a variety of theories as to its nature, its relationship to the body, and its origin and mortality. Soul is coined from the ancient Greek word, "psyche" which means "to breathe". Soul entails the mental abilities exhibited by a living being: reason, attitude, morals, feeling, consciousness, memory, perception etc. Depending on the philosophical system, a soul can either be mortal or immortal.

Ancient Greeks' notions of the soul differed significantly as indicated by the philosophical school. The Epicureans believed the soul to be comprised of atoms just like it's physical body counterpart. For the Platonists, the soul was a ghostly and spiritual substance, likened to the divine beings yet part of this world of the physical. For Aristotle, the concept of soul wasn't so certain, even though he admitted that it was a form indivisible from the body. Coming to Christian philosophy St. Augustine explained the soul to be a "rider" on the body, placing an obvious split between the material and the immaterial aspect of this world, with the soul being the "true" person. In any case, despite the fact that the body and soul were separate, it was impossible to conceive the idea of the soul without its body. In the Middle Ages, **St. Thomas Aquinas** came back to the Greek philosophers' concept of the soul as a driving force of the body, although it's independent, it still requires the substance of the body to make a person.

Starting from the Middle Ages, the presence and nature of the soul and its relationship to the body is still a matter of dispute among the Western philosophers. **René Descartes** was of the opinion that man is a union of the body and the soul, each existing as a distinct entity acting on the other; the soul could be likened to the mind. To **Benedict de Spinoza**, body and soul are dual aspects of a single reality. However, Immanuel Kant inferred that the soul was not an entity that could be proved through explanation, despite the fact that the mind necessarily has to arrive at the conclusion that the soul exists because such an idea was fundamental for the development of morals and religion. To **William James**, the concept of soul was just imaginary and a mere collection of psychic assumptions.

Similarly, as there have been various ideas of the connection of the soul to the body, there have been various ideas regarding when the soul comes into existence and when, if and how it dies. The beliefs of the Ancient Greeks about this differed and evolved with time. **Pythagoras** stated that the soul had a divine origin, and exists before and after the death of the body. **Plato and Socrates** additionally accepted the concept of the eternal status of the soul, while Aristotle was of the opinion that only a part of the soul called the noûs, or intellect, had that property. Furthermore, **"Epicurus"** was of the belief that both the body and the soul end at death. The early Christian philosophers embraced the Greek idea of the soul's immortality and thought of the spirit as being made by God and infused into the body at inception.

However, not all major religions adopt the concept of the eternal status of the soul, most table example about this is Buddhism. Buddhism does not deny the existence of "immaterial" entities, in fact, it traditionally distinguishes bodily states from mental states. Rather, Buddhism opposes the existence of a permanent entity that stays constant behind the changing bodily and ethereal segments of a living being. Just as the body transforms from time to time, thoughts come and go too, and there is no permanent state in the mind that experiences these considerations, as in Cartesianism.

Conscious mental states basically emerge and die with no "mastermind" behind them. When the physical body dies, Buddhists accept the divine mental processes continue and are reborn in another body. Because these mental processes are continually changing, the being that is reborn is neither totally different from nor exactly the same as, the being that died. However, the new being is continuous with the being that died, it's just like saying that the "you" of this present moment is continuous with the "you" of a past moment, even though you are continually changing, I know you're going to ask mummy numerous questions about this, just take it easy (Chuckles).

Do Animals Have Souls?

The soul is the principle of life. A number of philosophers are of the opinion that since animals and plants are living things, then they have souls, but their soulish characteristics differ from the one in human beings. The human soul is believed to be rational, while that of animals is said to be irrational. The human soul is rational because it is spiritual, not material. On the other hand, antagonists of the idea that animals have a soul are of the opinion that animals can't do anything which exceeds the limitations of matter. Although some animals seem clever, they don't actually possess convectional intelligence, take for example, animals can't come up with the abstract notion of justice.

A characteristic of any creature with soul is to have mental activities that consist of beliefs, intentions, desires, sensations, other activities that require mental reasoning and connection. The point being, anything that has beliefs, intentions, desires or sensations must also have a soul to possess those qualities. Furthermore, another belief is that animals possess different kinds of souls than human beings. As earlier stated, the souls of human beings are said to be eternal and immortal. On the other hand, there's no evidence that can tell whether animals have an eternal soul.

Take a look at these real life happenings:

-A blind Jack Russell has his very own guide dog and best friend, a Staffordshire terrier who accompanies him everywhere.

- A dairy cow was so sad from having previous calves taken away that she hid her newborn in a tall patch of grass.

-Willie the parrot alerted his human that her toddler was choking by crying out, "Mama, baby!"

-Two rescued circus elephants locked trunks and happily played together when they were reunited after 20 years apart.

-A female macaque named Positi rescued stray kittens and took care of them as if they were her own babies.

-Mila, a beluga whale, saved a drowning diver in China by pulling her to the surface so she could breathe.

-Scout the kitty lost her best friend, Charlie the dog, to cancer. Her owner puts an iPad on Charlie's dog bed and plays videos for the cat while she watches them and snuggles up to the screen.

What we observe in all these examples is the moral responsibility and connection which all these animals possess. In as much as they can choose to do good things, even to humans, is a visible proof that there is more to animals than the body alone.

Why are people scared to Die?

Death anxiety is anxiety brought upon us by the thoughts of death. Another definition sees death anxiety as a "feeling of terror, dread, unease when one thinks about the process of dying or the striking fear one has when one thinks about ceasing to exist. Death anxiety is generally referred to as "Thanatophobia" which is the fear of death. But why does this anxiety take hold of us? Why are we afraid of dying? One has every reason to believe that our point of view about death significantly depends on our background, the death experiences we've had over the years and our level of coping with things that happen. It is an obvious fact that this fear cannot be said to be caused by just a single factor. Death is subjective, similar to pain, it is the thought of the kind of death and the pain of dying that triggers this fear. Moreover, for someone whose personality is fragile, timid, weak, coupled with cold-feet experiences, all these add up to increase this fear. In a similar manner, to every unpleasant situation in an individual's life, the kind of death we've seen people have, our beliefs, life philosophy and other external influences we've had during our lifetime will confirm whether we have a fear towards death, or not.

Several observations have indicated that, the more people age, the more they adapt to the idea of death. This might be attributed to the fact that as we age, we tend to become more aware of our biological and environmental vulnerability, biological vulnerability as in terminal diseases, cancer, sickle cell anemia, age-related diseases such as hypertension, high blood pressure, natural death. Environmental vulnerabilities as car accidents, plane crash, home accidents, fire outbreak, natural disasters (earthquake, flood, disease outbreaks (At least, you know of the Corona Virus Disease!), and so on. What raises our level of fear about these things is the fact that there's little or nothing we can do to prevent them, hence we tend to develop this fear of hopelessness, with the idea of living life to it's fullest, after all. we're going leave one day.

There are numerous aspects about this phenomenon. We are excited about discovering what's beyond this world, what life exists after death, but at the same time, we're terrified about the idea of death, is it painful? Is it as peaceful as it seems? Is it truly a State of resting for eternity? But popular opinions think our concerns lie in the fact that we all can't escape it, but we just don't know what happens after we die or what awaits us, and that where our fear originates.

In as much as it is an established fact that a significant portion of the population are afraid of death which is understandable, there's still a large quota of us that are not frightened by this idea of death, probably because, at certain points of their lives, they've had experiences and seen things that gave them the conclusion that life is just a part of a journey and it's not the entire journey, therefore, death doesn't end anything. In fact, a person who previously had death anxiety might change to become indifferent about death, it all depends on our perspective and notion of life.

Furthermore, as biological entities, humans want to survive and the idea of leaving all they've achieved; everyone we've grown to know, everyone we care about, everyone who cares about us, all the wealth, all the fame, all that we enjoying doing, and everything we know, behind is unpleasant in our minds. Also, to some deep thinkers, being afraid of death is not limited to the reasons mentioned above, but because they feel they may not have enough time to accomplish all that they have on their minds. Another obvious reason is the fact that some people are afraid of the thought that they may end up having a painful death.

Although death has several negative sides, if people could live forever, would anyone actually appreciate and respect life? Assuming people didn't die, wouldn't they just sit all day in front of a TV doing nothing, because they would have in mind "I have endless time to do other things as well, let me just do nothing for now"?

Death is an important and sometimes an unexpected change, most individual resists the change. We are afraid because based on our instincts, we resist death because everything we've been doing to survive, most of our daily activities is to resist death. Come to think of it, when you were a baby, your parents would always guide you, feed you with the right food, take care of you just so that you don't harm yourself or become malnourished. The basic reason why we have jobs is to earn a living so we don't starve to death.

The master Chuang Tzu was of the opinion that man's thirst for survival in the future makes him incapable of living in the present and enjoying it. We bear an identity of ourselves inside us, based on our family, relationships, job, wealth, social image etc. Death erases this very foundation on which we build our identity, so we feel death snatches everything that is ours. Our understanding about death, or from another point of view, misunderstanding about death, makes death a fearful, frightening experience. A common school of thought would tell us that a man who resists death dies even while he lives, he dies every single time he is tortured by the very idea of death. Moreover, death in this context might not only mean physical death, Losing anything you care about is a form of death. Losing your comfortable life could be one form of death, losing your relatives is another.

When I die, where do I go?

In as much as the concept of life after death, paradise, heaven and hell are predominant, we really can't tell what happens to us or where we go after death. How can one be so certain about the afterlife? Even though from ancient times, people have placed their belief in the concept of the afterlife, and there's probably no means to tell that they're wrong or right. However, we can identify wishful thinking when we see it, and from that, an indifferent individual can say that people believe in the concept of the afterlife because the idea of dying isn't soothing to them. Hence, the afterlife concept provides them with a soothing fantasy. Contrarily, not all that is said about the afterlife is comforting, not all perspectives will tell you that the afterlife is a place of rest, peace, no suffering, no death, no pain, not everyone will be of that opinion, at least Williams Shakespeare's Hamlet wasn't.

 Looking at it from a religious point of view, we are left with the concept of heaven and hell, which appears to be two sides of a coin. Heaven is one flip side, it is the place your soul goes after your death if while you were alive, you obeyed God's commandments, you did good, you were kind, then God welcomes your soul into his heavenly abode. On the other hand, hell, which is the other side of the flip is where your soul goes if you did not finish well on earth before you died. Even though no one has met anyone from the afterlife or any of these concepts, believing in the afterlife is not by virtue of evidence it's a concept that people hold on to by virtue of their faith, at least for the time being while we're here.

Let's assume I told you that some really interesting stuffs are happening in a really amazing – but far off – place. No doubt, you and I are missing out on all the fun and enjoyment. Despite the fact that i haven't been to this place, you don't have any basis to deny the existence of this cool place, just because it's not nearby, or because it's not part of the here and now. In a similar manner, You don't have any basis to believe and promote it either. What then? Well, suppose I make up my that I'm going to go find out the truth for myself. I'm going on a journey to find this really cool place. Would you be willing to follow me? Maybe not – but wouldn't you even be the least bit curious? Wouldn't you want to know if I found it? Wouldn't you want to know what it's really like, if it's actually there? Let's say I embark on the journey, I found this really cool place, and If I made it back and told you about it, you'd probably be happy to listen and learn. So at least I've increased your curiosity. But, of course, as we all know, whatever lies beyond death is a one-way trip. If you really want to know, you've got to make that journey yourself.

Then again, denying the existence of an afterlife doesn't have to be about cowardice as opposed to courage – after all, everyone's going to make this journey one way or the other. And some of the several visions of what the afterlife might be like may be more reasonable and more persuasive than others.

Ethics

What is good? and what is bad?

The term " Good and Bad" is a very common dichotomy, that is to say, they are branches of the same tree. If what you're doing doesn't fall under the good branch, then it definitely falls under the bad branch. Talking about the Manichaean and Abrahamic religious influence, evil/bad is generally perceived as the dualistic opposite of good, in which good is expected to be dominant and the evil or bad side should be defeated. In this context, I'll mostly use the word " Evil" in place of the word "Bad". Do take note that I'm referring to the same thing. Evil, in a general circumstance, is the absence of that which is generally accepted to be good, it is driven by fear, immoral intentions and manifests through a secretive means, violence, force, or without knowledge of the person being affected.

Philosophers of different ages and origins have pondered on this question. Each thought that he had provided sufficient answers to the question once and for all, yet within a few years, the problem would come up again bearing another dimension. In fact, most of the answers would be later found inadequate or unsatisfactory. Religious thinkers also joined in presenting a solution to this long-lasting problem, however, in an attempt to do so, they made things more complex. Some other basic questions that needed to be answered in order to generate an acceptable answer were:

- Is the notion and knowledge of good and evil inborn in the nature of man or has he been given divine directives? If not, how does one identify what is good from what is bad? If our sense of reasoning is the only way to distinguish, is there any laid-down to determine what is good and what is evil?

- If good and bad are separate entities, are they from the same creator? Or is God the Creator of good alone? If so, where does "Bad" originate from? Who created evil?

- If the knowledge of good and evil is inborn and instinctive, there should be uniformity of thought among the different nations, religions and groups of the world, but what we have is vast differences among these categories in almost every aspect. Why?

Thomas Hobbes was of the opinion that good and evil are relative. According to him, they are dynamic, they change not only with time but with every individual as well; that which seems to please man is good, and that which causes pain, suffering or discomfort for man is bad. Bearing in mind that what pleases one person may not please the other, therefore, there is no entirely good or bad. Take for example, you as a 10-year old, your favorite thing is ice-cream right? Good, it gives you that satisfaction, it gives you a sweet feeling that makes you want more, it pleases you. But if you save your money and buy an ice-cream for your Granny on her 85th birthday, she'll only thank you but she won't accept it from you. Don't be sad, of course, Granny loves you, it's just that taking an ice cream is probably bad for her health at that age. Do we say an ice cream is good? or Do we say it is bad? The concept of good or bad is dynamic and changes with time and person.

Socrates, the great Greek Philosopher, thought that one of the most vital and complex questions before man is the recognition of good and bad. According to him, knowledge of good and bad, as well as its criteria are inbuilt in man and he can differentiate between the two if he wants to. With prolonged thought and guidance of nature he is capable of knowing what is good and what is evil. His popular saying `O man! Know thyself' also tells us that the basic principles of good and evil are innate in man and can be discovered by deliberate acts and choices. Socrates had a rigid view that there should be basic principles independent of individual choices and beliefs for determining good and bad, right and wrong. Socrates stated that "No man is voluntarily bad.' He turns bad when he cannot separate what is good from what is evil, based on the circumstances he finds himself in and the decisions he makes. If he had an idea of what he was sure to choose it.'

Plato thought that man is blessed with the knowledge of good and evil before coming to this world. This knowledge existed in his soul but during the period between his creation and his descent in this world, however, he forgot most of the things. These forgotten principles can be regained either by wise sermons, teachings, through experience or through meditation on nature. All good and evil are innate in man. To Plato, good itself is happiness.

A Christian thinker of the middle ages, Peter Abelard, added a new dimension to the problem. According to Peter, an act itself is not good or bad but it is the intention of the person that does it hat makes it good or bad. If a thief commits a theft intending it as something good, it is thereby good. God takes into account only the spirit in which an act is done. If carries out an act because he thinks that is the right thing to do but errs and does wrong, the act will remain good. According to him, goodness and morality are a subject of conscience and intention to do wrong. An evil that is committed with good intention in mind is not sinful, as anything that is bad is sinful. Another Christian thinker, Thomas Aquinas, also agreed with the concept that goodness or evil of a particular action depends upon the aim or intention of the doer.

However, he had a different view from Abelard's view that a bad act if done with a good intention becomes good. According to him, a good act is that which is done with good intentions and with the just the mere knowledge that the results would be good. He said that God has created all things including man for good. Achieving goodness is the ultimate good, and the best way to attain goodness is to abandon worldly things and make efforts to have communion with God like a saint in a monastery devoting himself entirely to the service of God. For Aquinas, evil is the negation of good. Where there is no good, there is evil there is no two way about it. For him, evil is the absence of good. When an object fails to achieve good results, evil comes into being.

Immanuel Kant, however, held that the concept of good and bad are well known since eternity and the moral laws are inborn in man's nature and intellect. One of these laws that serve as a criterion for setting apart what is good from what is bad, this is the law that says one should like for others what he likes for himself. Kant opposed the principle that an act is good if its result is good. He stated that the consequences of an act do not define the characteristics of that act. If the act is carried out with good intentions out of respect for moral laws it is thereby good. He ended his words by saying always do what everybody would like to follow.'

Another Philosopher, Spinoza, also considered good and evil to be relative. In fact, there is neither good nor evil in the universe nor is it essential. We have partial knowledge about things, in spite of this, we want that everything should happen according to the way we reason them or the way we want them to be and when it happens otherwise, it looks to be bad. What appears to our intellect to be bad to us might not be so according to nature's law, it is bad judging by the laws that relate to us. Similarly, everything that helps man to achieve the goal of his struggle is good and that tending to block this struggle is bad. According to Spinoza, an act can be good and bad at the same time and be devoid of them both as well. For example, a happy man enjoys playing music but a grieved and sorrowful man does not like it. For the dead, it is neither good nor bad. To Spinoza good and evil, are based on the mindset that cannot be recognized.

What is the difference between good and bad?

The first thing we must think about in order to distinguish between good acts and bad acts is that good acts are acts that can be improved upon by the doer and acts that can be improved by the circumstances surrounding the person. Let's take a look at a case whereby two good acts can be compared and one is better than the other, a traditional healer in a tribal village may treat a person complaining of stomach pains a plant to chew on that reduces his pain. On the long run, the patient travels to an urban society and is examined by a modern doctor were and diagnosis shows that the person has another digestive illness which was most likely caused by the plants the traditional healer gave him, the doctor carries out surgery on the patient and he's healed. The doctor's act was better than the traditional healer's act, however, this doesn't imply that the what the traditional healer did was bad, what he did was with the good intention of healing the patient of stomach ache, which he did, he wasn't aware of the side effects. However, from that point onward, after being told that the plants cause other diseases, if he keeps on giving it to people to use, that's a bad act.

The second thing we should consider is the ultimate intention of an act. Suppose someone decides to steal some loaves of bread from the local store. He stole them because it was the easiest way to satisfy his hunger at the time, to keep himself alive. He satisfies his hunger because he needs to eat. So the ultimate intention of stealing those loaves of bread is preserving his life. The proximate intentions are stealing those loaves of bread and satisfying his hunger.

When an act is evil, the ultimate intention ceases to be carried out consistently. If the thief keeps on stealing all in the name of trying to survive without doing anything that is generally acceptable to help his situation, he is despising the owner of the things in the store, it has become a morally bad act. Nonetheless, his ultimate intention to preserve his own life is undercut by his means of carrying it out. Even though it preserves his life, it has become habitual and normal to him, and hence bad. So this is consistent with my earlier analysis of good and evil.

Another belief is that good, bad, all seem to be evaluative terms. They are terms that express commendation or disapproval, and simply evaluative situations based on the 'criterion' that we have. The term " good" can be used in a functional sense, i.e. something is good because it serves its purpose. A bike could be good because it serves its function, it is a means of transport, its brakes work, the tires aren't flat. It might be a good commuter bike but a bad racing bike. We evaluate a bike with respect to the function it has.

"Good", in contrary to "evil' is just based on moral evaluation, and it is different from the functional evaluation made earlier. There is something different about saying "This is a good car." and "It is good to attain your goals". Although, "good" in the moral sense is also evaluative but that the evaluation is made with respect to a specific "criterion" and that "criterion" is whatever promotes human progress and happiness and in this sense, "Bad" is that which doesn't promote human progress and happiness.

Do Animals have a Concept of good and bad?

In terms of moral philosophy, what spot should non-human creatures occupy in a satisfactory moral system? These creatures exist on the borderline of our ethical ideas; the outcome is that we at times end up agreeing to their solid moral status, while at different times denying them any sort of moral status whatsoever. For instance, the outrage is much when information about puppy mills which are "little dog factories" is made known to the public. Puppy mills are similar to puppy farms which serve as commercial dog breeding factories attributed to quick breeding but predominant poor environmental conditions. The idea here is that dogs should be given better considerations by the operators of such mills. Philosophical speculation on the ethical status of animals is different and can be commonly grouped into three general classes: Indirect theory, direct but unequal theory, and moral equity theory.

Talking about indirect theory, this denies creatures moral status or equivalent consideration with humans because of the absence of consciousness, reason, or independence. Ultimately disproving the moral status of these creatures, theories under the indirect theory may even include not hurting creatures, simply because doing so mars the individual's morality. Arguments in this class have been proposed by several philosophers, including Immanuel Kant, René Descartes, Thomas Aquinas, Peter Carruthers, and different strict hypotheses.

On the other hand, direct yet unequal theory accords some ethical considerations to animals yet deny them a more full moral status because of their inability to regard one another's rights or show moral correspondence inside a community of equivalent animals. However, where the interests of creatures and people strife, the extraordinary properties of being human, for example, judiciousness, self-governance, and hesitance accord, give higher thought to the interests of individuals.

Finally, the moral equity theory extends equivalent consideration and moral status to creatures by disproving the alleged moral relevance of the previously mentioned extraordinary properties of human beings. Arguing by relationship, theories about moral equality frequently stretch out the idea of rights to creatures in light of the fact that they have similar physiological and intellectual abilities as babies or crippled individuals.

Furthermore, the concept of good or bad is a complex idea to characterize. Frequently, we consider human ethics as far as our common laws and religious rules, it's the same as saying they are things we disobey only to bring common punishments upon ourselves. In this sense, we can't verify that animals have morals or a guiding principle to know what's good or bad, because either ways, there's no reward or punishment.

However, there is an impressive logical writing on " Animal politics," " Animal morals", and so forth, because certain animals, particularly primates like us, show certain behaviors aimed at winning or retaining kindness of their social mates, to secure about socially advantageous acts of equal kindness, etc., and to connive against Intruders of this social contract. Examples of this include sharing of food among chimpanzees and monkeys, and mandrills helping each other out in some form of alliances.

To go beyond primates, even in vampire bats, a female will share food with a friend to save the friend's life after a night or two of unsuccessful hunting, and usually, the friend will reciprocate at other times; but when an individual fails to reciprocate, others become more reluctant to come to her aid. Through the cold calculus of death, natural selection can therefore work against selfishness and in favor of generosity and reciprocation. Permit me to bring some instances back into this, these are real life cases where animals made choices of either doing what's good or bad:

-A blind Jack Russell has his very own guide dog and best friend, a Staffordshire terrier who accompanies him everywhere.

-A female macaque named Positi rescued stray kittens and took care of them as if they were her own babies.

-Mila, a beluga whale, saved a drowning diver in China by pulling her to the surface so she could breathe.

-Scout the kitty lost her best friend, Charlie the dog, to cancer. Her owner puts an iPad on Charlie's dog's bed and plays videos for the cat while she watches them and snuggles up to the screen

Therefore, humans are not the only species to have a social contract based on mutual trust, aid-giving, and reciprocation. This appears to be a fundamental instinct in certain other animals as well, and arguably, our civil laws and religious beliefs are themselves products of evolution that function to codify and enforce these prehistoric, preliterate moral codes.

How do Our Actions Affect Other People?

To have an impact is the action of one object coming forcefully into contact with another. Speaking of relationships, it denotes a person's actions having an influence on others. There's a general saying that you attract the energy you put out., It's like Soka throwing his boomerang in Avatar: Legend of Aang animation, it always comes back to him. You treat others the way you want to be treated by others. Your personality and behavior can have influence a person positively or negatively, it influences their behavior, their actions, their views about life, their mentality, and even their attitudes. However, an individual may not have any idea of how his or her attitude or the impact it is causing on behavior.

A leader or teammate who shows encouraging and positive attitudes towards followers, teammates or co-workers can positively influence those in close association with them. As a matter of fact, those bright smiles of yours can be a significant input in someone's day. That friendly attitude you portray has the power to be contagious and spread fast. Your generosity can be the one thing that puts a smile on people's faces. Your compassion can be all that will draw that fellow out of depression, and surprisingly, you might not even know!

People's behaviors can also be a deficiency, not only for the person carrying out such behaviors but also for others around such an individual. Your energy or conduct towards other people if negative, could draw negative people to you. An unhappy person has the ability to attract other unhappy individuals if such an individual isn't careful. Research has shown that an unpleasant attitude or a mean, negative behavior could ultimately have a negative effect on your day to day functions. It could have unimaginable legal and financial consequences and can as well be the cause of mental health issues such as depression, which might eventually originate thoughts of suicide. Negative mindset, behavior and attitude towards things have powerful effects than we think they do.

Reflect upon the people in your life and the type of friends you hang around with. You might be able to notice the relationship between the way you choose to treat others and the type and amount of friends that you have. Make a conscious effort to choose your attitude so that you can impact how your relationship with others flourishes. Every day, do your possible best to be there for someone and do not let it affect your personal life because you can't afford to be sad while you're trying to make others happy. Whether it's your classmates, football teammates, that girl you go to the Bailey dance together, that boy that seems not to understand mathematics in your class, that pretty girl you're crushing on but likes to always be alone (winks) and most importantly, your relatives. Make each and everyday count.

An important thing to remember is that the impact you have on others, by the actions or words you share, are what people will remember you by. You definitely don't want to be that boy that grows up to hate his dad or uncle, however, this is predominant in the society today. On numerous occasions, the words and remarks of parents have been the reason their children gave up, the reason they stopped trying, the reason they think they can never get a good grade, the reason they think they'll never be great in life. And in certain circumstances, a soft pat on the head while whispering to the child " You can do it boy", has been the reason the children buckled up, the reason they started improving academically from that day. The family is the first school of life, the behaviors of the father and the mother have been the deciding factor of the children's behavior. You can't expect a drunkard to advise his son not to drink.

As a matter of fact, the family heavily influences the behavior of the children to the outside world. A home where the father maltreats the mother and the children, one can't expect such children to bear a positive attitude to the outside world. They're somewhat depressed, and if they're not careful, they'll attract unhappy people too and the circle goes on and on, meanwhile, it all started with the actions of the father.

"My sweet mother's funeral, even though I was not very engaged I must admit, I do recall so many people attending...each one of them sharing small and grand gestures she had bestowed on each of them. So many stories from my mom baking a pie or cake for them. Countless stories of helping others. Countless stories of unselfish acts. Immeasurable narratives of feeding individual people and families alike. So people did not remember what she had, they recalled her actions and gestures she shared- the impact she made in their lives." This is the story of a man who had a loving grandma who influenced people in the society with her little act of sharing things. To her it was just a mere cheerful behavior, to other people, she was a mentor.

If I punch Someone because He punched Me first, does it make Me a bad Person

So this is a scenario in which you're in a heated argument with a boy and one thing led to another, then he punched you. You, being annoyed and enraged at that moment, you know responding with a punch would lead to a fight, a part of you wants to let things go, the other part feels you not responding means you've been cheated, that other part feels you have to make things leveled, you have to fight back! And everyone hates being cheated, so what did you do? You listened to that other part and punched him.

Compare this scenario with these real life stories:

During a U.S bomb combat operations in Iraq, a boy named Ali lost his arms, his parents, siblings, and several other relatives in the attack. The image of a boy who was injured, wounded, burned and yelling in pain on a hospital bed moved people around the globe to raise money for his medical care and further annoyed those who opposed the attack. A few months later, after Ali had been fitted for prosthetic arms at a London hospital, Ali made it known that he wished the people responsible for his misdemeanor and the loss of his family would feel the same kind of pain he was feeling. In his words, he said he hoped that the pilot who hit their house would be burned as he and his family were burned".

Second story: A boy and a girl who were classmates in primary school happened to be good friends too. They played shares things with each other and did things in common. One afternoon, during their plays as usual, the girl mistakenly tore a little portion of the boy's book, the boy was very much aware that it was a mistake, instead of looking over it, he decided he was going to do the same to the girl's book. So he told the girl to bring out one of her notes so he could tear a little part and make things leveled. The girl in disbelief thought her dear friend was joking, but he insisted, so she brought out a note and gave to him and to her amazement, he tore a little part. He had satisfied his intentions and rage, but that act forever affected their friendship.

Each of these circumstances can only be summed up with one word, Revenge!

In Ali's story, every word there drives us to one end, which is the need for vengeance. If he knew the pilot and he was capable, he would carry out his revenge at all costs.

We have all felt that way too, we have all been wronged by someone, it's either that spoilt daughter of your principal, that bully at school, the rude driver, and we have all felt the need to do to other people what they did to us. Even though the quest for revenge is normal and understandable, it is said to be unhealthy. Revenge is likened to hate because it takes over a person to feel offended. It takes a psychological and physical toll on such an individual, making him/her express those feelings of anger, which sometimes doesn't decrease the feeling. The thoughts of revenge eats us up if we do not take care of it. It becomes something one nurtures and grows in his/her mind.

The question whether you're a bad or good person lies behind the intention of your actions and revenge. People who revenge are often led by violence and anger and the need to express their negative feeling and rage. Therefore, from a significant perspective, returning that punch makes you a bad person who can't contain his feelings (at that moment) because the actions that will follow after that punch are much painful than a punch. However, not returning the punch would have probably settled the argument and brought in peace, which is the attribute of a good person, based on that circumstance.

Is it disrespectful if I disagree with My Parents or Teachers?

When you were much younger, your parents made every decision for you, from the food you eat to the clothes you put on, the school you attend, the time you play, the time you watch TV, and even the time you go to bed. However, as you grow up, the amount of decisions they make on your behalf reduces you now choose the clothes you'll put on to school, you decide the type of friends you have, and so on, and so forth. However, you'll get to a stage whereby you want to make all your decisions all by yourself, this is the adolescent stage. At this stage, you feel you're an adult and you deserve to be treated as one, however, your parents see you as a child who's growing and still needs to believe guided and mentored into the world of adulthood, this is where the contention comes in. At this stage, you might disagree with your parents on certain occasions and in really serious ones, you might disrespect them.

Bear in mind that there's a difference between disagreement and disrespectful. It is possible that you as a teenager, you respectfully disagree with your parents during an argument or conversation, if you disagree politely, it doesn't imply disrespect or disobedience, rather it reflects the fact that you're becoming an independent thinker.

Even your parents are aware of the fact that you can not always be on the same page in everything. However, do not ignore the fact that your parents are the adults in the room with more years of experience. The manner in which you present your point is what shows whether you're disagreeing with your parents or teachers, or you're disrespecting them. If you're yelling at them while talking or using foul words, it shows utmost disrespect. However, if you present your points and state your reasons calmly and politely, they'll even be convinced to agree with you. Teens need to learn to express their opinions in a logical, thoughtful, respectful way. To ensure that the conversation stays respectful, you try as much as possible to refrain from personal insults, accusations, or making the discussion one-sided. You and your parents should each focus on your opinions, explaining why you think the way you do, and listening to what the other has to say.

If I do bad things with good intentions, does that make me a Bad person?

In situations like this, we have to look at it in two ways, which are how you see yourself and how people see you. In any case, you're the only one who knows your intentions, other people and the people affected don't know, to them, all that matters is the outcome. But is it your inner motives that matter? Actually, No. To other people, to the witnesses and victims, what defines you are results. How can you even be sure that other people know what you're thinking, your intentions and knowing that you mean well? Even amongst a group of friends, arguments often arise due to the slightest bit of misunderstanding, why would you not expect the same with strangers?

Take a look at this example, Let's say a guy bought a gift for his close female friend on her birthday that he thought she would absolutely love cherish. However, this gift turned out to be something that triggered her to remember a sad day in her life, a damaging memory from her past that she's been trying to forget. Should she go ahead and accept the gift, reject it, or dispose of it? The guy was only trying to be friendly by presenting her with a gift on her birthday, however, it did not turn out that way, his act of kindness put the girl in a bad mood at that moment, does this make him a bad person?

In any association between two individuals, groups or sort there are going to be several interactions, all bearing an immeasurable weight of intentions. Those intentions are bound to change from interaction to interaction and be interpreted (or misinterpreted) based on the receiver's mood or disposition at that moment. What's even more crucial is that outcomes are external and it's what people know. It doesn't matter if you didn't intend to hit that pet dog with your car, what matters is the fact that you did. You were a driver with good intentions, but now you've killed a pet dog. What are you going to do about it? You can try to adjust your driving (pay more attention, drive slower, etc.), or you can blame the pet dog(shouldn't have been there in the first place). Nevertheless, it happened, irrespective of your intentions, and now you get to choose how to move on.

Lying

Sometimes ago, there was a case which involved a politician, he publicly claimed that he had never looked into people's life before or dug into their past. However, before the end of the day, the people he hired to do such acts, came clean and confessed openly. What does that make the politician become? A Liar! Definitely, It wasn't the first time a politician lied and it won't be the last. Sometimes a lie, which is a false statement made with deliberate intent to deceive, turns out to be the perfect response: a brother lies about his sister's where-about to the maltreating husband intending to harm her, a doctor tells a depressed patient that he has an equal chance of recovery when she knows the patient has only six months left to live he, a son gives his late mother's estate to the poor after promising to honor her demand that the money be placed in her coffin.

When you make efforts to do the right thing in a difficult situation, perfect honesty may seem the second-best line of action next to values like compassion, respect, and justice. However, several philosophical and religious traditions have long claimed that rarely, if ever, is a lie acceptable. What, then, is the truth about lying?

Immanuel Kant was of the opinion that lying is always morally wrong. He argued that all human beings are born with an "intrinsic worth" that he referred to as human dignity. This dignity one obtains due to the fact humans are uniquely rational agents, who are capable of making decisions freely by themselves, setting their targets, and directing their conduct by reason. According to Kant, to be human is to possess the rational power of free choice; to be ethical, is to acknowledge and respect that power in oneself and others.

Lies are morally wrong for certain reasons. First, lying corrupts the vital qualities of being human: your ability to make free, rational choices. Each lie one tells contradicts the part of me that gives you a moral worth. Second, lies deny others of their freedom to choose rationally. When my lie causes people to make the wrong decisions which they wouldn't have made if they knew the truth, I have tainted their human dignity and Independence. Kant believed that to value ourselves, in other words, we have perfect duties to avoid damaging, interfering with, or abusing the ability to make free decisions; that is to say, no lying.

Another perspective is virtue ethics, which also holds that lying is morally wrong, though less strictly than Kant. Rather than judge right or wrong behavior on the basis of reason and what people should or should not do, virtue ethicists focus on the development of character or what people should be. Virtues are desirable qualities of persons that predispose them to act in a certain manner. Fairness, for example, is a virtue we may choose to strive toward in pursuit of fulfilling our human potential. In virtue ethics, to be virtuous is to be ethical. Though the outlook of virtue ethics makes it complex to assess the morality of individual acts, those who proposed this theory generally view lying as a morally wrong act because it opposes the virtue of honesty. However, there are instances whereby a lie is told in pursuit of another virtue, for instance, compassion: the brother's lie to his sister's drunken husband is motivated by compassion for her physical safety), is that morally right or wrong?

Moving to the third perspective which is utilitarian ethics, Kant and virtue ethicists ignore the only condition necessary for judging the morality of a lie, which is weighing the benefits and harms of its consequences. Utilitarians base their reasoning on the claim that actions, including lying, are morally acceptable when the resulting consequences maximize benefit or minimize harm. A lie, therefore, is not immoral at all times, in fact, when lying is necessary to maximize benefit or minimize harm, it may be considered immoral if you do not lie. The challenge in applying utilitarian ethics to everyday decision making, however, is significant: one must correctly think of the overall consequences of one's actions before making a decision. For instance, remember the son and his dying mother mentioned earlier, on careful reflection, the son thinks that honoring his mother's request to settle the estate and deposit the money in her coffin cannot be the right thing to do even though that was her wish. The money would be wasted or possibly stolen and the poor would be denied an opportunity to benefit. Knowing that his mother would ask someone else to carry out the task if he said he wasn't going to fulfill her last wish, he lies by falsely promising to honor her request. Utilitarianism, in this sense, supports the son's decision on the determination that the greater good will be achieved if he lied.

Stealing

Initially, this may appear to be like a fairly simple thing to do; stealing is just the taking of another person's property without the person's consent. Definitely, if reality television probably programs following Traffic Police are to accept any definition, that would be the definition. However, this definition is of use not merely for philosophy classes, but for the real world also; theft of vehicles is often categorized as an example of TWOC — "taking without owners' consent."

However, it is not always clear that stealing comfortably satisfies this definition. For example, we might wonder if it is possible to steal an item even though the owner has given you consent to take it. The original definition would say this is wrong and rule this out as an impossibility, but consider someone who, while intoxicated or perhaps high on drugs against their will, gives you permission to take an item of value from their house. Even though you have their permission, acting on this verbal instruction and stealing their laptop still might be said to be an act of theft.

Another opposing example to the original definition, imagine that you are better at cards than someone else, although you hide this fact from them. If you play a game for real money and beat them in each round, can one jump into a conclusion that you have stolen their money even though they entered into the game out of their conscious free will?

There are responses to these two examples, of course. We might deny that either of these examples is an act of stealing, or deny that proper consent was ever given (especially in the first example). However, we can also direct our doubts on the definition by focusing not on the issue of consent, but the idea of property. For example, if a person is being paid by the hour, but spends an undue amount of time on social media or checking sports scores, have they stolen money or time from their employer? Or, as a second possible example, if I make up a joke that is then retold by someone else, have they stolen "joke" without my consent? This is a genuinely important issue in the field of comedy, for example. Furthermore, consider the example of someone who fails to pay their legally due portion of tax to the government. Again, we might wonder if this person has "stolen" money just by refusing to hand over their financial property. If so, our reading of the original definition of stealing would again need to be rather broad. All of this has hopefully opened your minds to the variety of acts that may or may not be labeled as stealing.

Utilitarian theories, which entails Act, Rule, and Preference, are connected by their commitment to the view that it is a consequence of an action that determines its morality, although the three theories have slightly different views on how this central claim should be interpreted in practice.

Take a look at these instances:

James can illegally download a music album that he would derive satisfaction from, saving himself money in doing so. Or, he can pay full price for the music and allow his money to line the pockets of an international pop star, and her wealthy producer. In this case, more pleasure would seem to be produced by an illegal download rather than a paid-for download

Katie and Matt are going to miss a concert that they have been looking forward to for a very long time because their car has broken down. By chance, they notice an unlocked car parked on a driveway near them. If they steal the car, attend the concert, refill it with petrol and park it back on the driveway — all without the owner's knowledge — then their action appears to provide them with a great deal of pleasure and no pain at all to the actual owner of the car.

James has two children who are desperate for a particular Christmas present. If he steals the present, which he cannot afford to buy, from a major international retailer then this action would very likely lead to far more pleasure for his children than pain for the company.

Thus, even when we might think an individual act of stealing will produce the maximum amount of pleasure in a given situation, we should be wary of over-confidence in our analysis, and not downplay the painful consequences associated with that possible action. Act and preference Utilitarians may make their final stand on this issue by suggesting that greater attention should be paid to the psychological costs associated with stealing. The pain of a victim will not be fully accounted for if we only think of immediate pains to do with finance and anger. In addition, we must recognize the psychological pain often resulting from the fear of having property stolen or a house burgled. This psychological distress may be so severe that it outweighs even large-scale pleasures resulting from the theft. In addition, it might be the case that engaging in an act of stealing in one potentially morally justifiable situation would make someone more prone to stealing in a second, or third or fourth situation where moral legitimacy is either more questionable or obviously not present.

Cheating

Some questions are of particular interest when it comes to cheating: What is cheating? Is it something other than breaking a rule? Is every breaking of a rule an instance of cheating? It doesn't seem to be the case. And, is the concept of cheating referring to similar in acts in different instances; so for instance, is cheating in sport different in any morally significant way from cheating on your taxes, or on your spouse, or in an exam? And how is it defined in each of these instances? Let's be detailed about cheating in sports.

 If we're to define cheating in sports, on what basis do we do that? There are a few ways to do so, but each brings its own set of issues. First, we could say that cheating occurs when one intentionally breaks the rules. So, if I purposefully do something contrary to the rules, I have cheated. But this definition doesn't seem to be absolutely true. If I purposefully foul someone in order to stop them from scoring, say in basketball, then I cheat? On this view it seems that I do. This seems wrong to me. Certainly I commit a foul, but committing a foul seems much different than cheating. What seems more like cheating is committing a foul, then acting as if I did not commit the foul by deceiving the refs and crowd into thinking that no foul was committed. Or maybe I cheat if I commit a foul and don't tell others that I have committed the foul. In the latter case, I am trying to get away with something that is against the rules and that seems to add a component to the original formulation of cheating that rings more intuitive to my ears. This added statement seems to be an instance of deception.

But to further press on the initial formulation, intentionally breaking the rules isn't always bad, is it? Consider a case where I intentionally break a rule to even the playing field for the other team. Let's say I commit a foul, and no one notices but it turns out that committing that foul would win us the game if I do not do anything about the situation. To make up for my unfair play, I break another rule, but this time I intentionally break a rule in order to give the other team another shot at tying the game. It seems commendable for me to do this and not at all like cheating. So it can't be that cheating occurs when we intentionally break the rules. But for those who will agree to the formulation, then there will be at least two kinds of cheating, moral and immoral cheating and this seems odd given that cheating seems to be something immoral by its very nature.

For you, the most common form of cheating you'll probably have experienced is with your friends or classmate. Probably you both agreed to do something, and after fulfilling your part of the deal, he refuses to fulfill his, that's dishonesty, that's deceitful, and that's cheating! You may never trust such a person again or have anything to do with him. However, if at a later time, you cheat on him too, that's immoral and is based on revenge. Cheating is simply taking advantage of another person, trying to outsmart them or play on their intelligence. However, if cheating is immoral, then it is immoral whether you cheat on a saint or a scoundrel.

What is Conscience?

Conscience is a personal sense of the moral rightness of one's mode of conduct, intentions, or character with regard to a feeling of responsibility to do right or be good at all times. Our conscience is usually influenced by what we have grown to know, the instructions we've been given. It Is therefore generally understood to give naturally authoritative judgments regarding the moral concept of our actions. If we go further, we can define conscience as an inward-looking character, in the following ways: conscience is always the knowledge of ourselves, or we being aware of moral principles that we are committed to, or assessment of ourselves, or motivation to act that comes from within us with no external influence.

Conscience is an aspect of the mind that encourages us to act morally or at least to act according to our most deeply held values. Many people are of the opinion that it is a form of natural knowledge and involves emotion, although general opinions suggest that it should be shaped by proper reasoning. It is a personal experience and a form of self-knowledge. From your conscience, you can come up with your own values and morals. It might interest you to know that the word " conscience" has a Latin origin which is con-scientia and one of the ways to translate it is "together-with-knowing", in other words, to be together with one's knowledge, in this case, one's knowledge of morality.

Through our individual conscience, we get to know our highly esteemed moral principles, we are motivated to act upon them, and we examine our character, our behavior and most importantly, ourselves against those principles. Different philosophical, religious and common-sense approaches to conscience have come up with different aspects of this word with broad application.

In terms of religion, most religions believe that the morality that influences our conscience does or should come from either God or an enlightened mind. Furthermore, among different religions, there are different concepts as to whether conscience is seen mainly as a punishment or as a virtue we should embrace. Philosophically, several philosophers have adopted the concept, which states that a truly moral conscience requires the exercise of reason; others have claimed that it is an intuition of objective moral truth. Early philosophers seemed to believe in a natural and objective morality definition of conscience, something like a truly moral instinct. Modern philosophers tend to recognize the cultural and individual relativity of morality, and many present arguments based on scientific theories about mind, evolution, and society.

Legally, the law states that we have the right to "freedom of conscience," this tells us that we should be free to obey our consciences, but within limits. Considering that we don't have a clear or unified philosophy of conscience, this raises legal, political, and social issues. However, popular opinion, which talks about our everyday notions of conscience are philosophically interesting. Consider that conscience is a part of us opposing actions that we ourselves view to be immoral, but are in danger of doing anyway. It seems a little self-opposing, but Why do we even need a conscience?

Outside the realm of religion, philosophers, social scientists, and psychologists have sought to understand conscience in both its individual and universal nature. The view that holds conscience to be an innate, natural sense that determines the perception of right and wrong, this is referred to as intuitionism. It's just like this, every afternoon you buy an ice-cream from the kiosk guy, each ice-cream costs $5, which you are very much aware of. This day, the kiosk guy is so busy attending to a lot of customers and because he knows you as a regular buyer, he sees you and decides to quickly attend to you.

Let's assume you went there with $20 and you bought 2 ice-creams, common expectation is that you should collect two ice-creams and a balance of $10 in return, however, because he's in a haste, the seller mistakenly gives you $15, and tells you bye! After taking few steps away from the kiosk, you decide to check the change and you find out that you've been given more than the right amount, do you ignore it and see it as an act of luck? Do you see it as an act of cheating and return it? What you do next solely depends on you, your morals, and whether you have the right conscience.

The view that sees conscience to be a judgement from past experiences giving direction to future conduct is called empiricism. The behavioral scientist, on the other hand, may view the conscience as a set of learned responses to particular social actions. Views about conscience are so diverse and complex that a one-way definition is not possible. This seems to be another paradox about conscience; we know it most intimately in ourselves, but there is no general agreement about where it comes from, or how much it should be respected.

What Are My Obligations to My Parents?

You Ought to Love Your Parents

LOVE is the only quality from which all other duties that you owe your parents can be carried out. By love, we mean affection; and surely every good father and mother deserve this. If you seem not to care about this, if you are without any attraction towards them, you are in a strange and guilty state of mind. Until you are married, or you are looking forward to, they ought, in most cases, to be the priority of your earthly affections. It is not enough for you to be respectful and obedient and even kind; but, you should also be fond of them. It is of great importance that you should watch over the internal state of your mind and not allow dislike, isolation, or indifference, to consume your love towards your parents. Do not take up a negative attitude against them, nor allow an unfavorable impression to be made upon your mind. If the respect and obedience you have for them do not spring from love, then they are valueless in their nature.

If you love your parents, you will be happy to be in their company, and take pleasure in being at home with them. It is somehow painful for them to see that you are happier anywhere than at home, and fonder of any other society than theirs. No companion should be so valued than the company of your father or mother. If you love them, you will ensure that you please them in all things because we are always anxious to please those whom we love and to avoid whatever would give them an unpleasant view about us. If we are careless, whether we please or displease any particular person, it is nearly impossible that we can have any affection for that person.

You ought to Respect and obey your parents

You should have high thoughts of their superiority, both natural and instituted, and submission of the heart to their authority, in the way of sincere and total respect. In fact, even the love you have for them must be that which is expressed towards a superior. If there be no respect of the heart, it cannot be expected in the conduct. In all virtue, whether it be that higher kind which has respect to God, or that secondary type of respect, which relates to our fellow human beings, we must have a right state of mind because without this, virtue does not exist. Your words should correspond with the respectful feelings of your mind. When speaking to them, your manner of approach, both in language and in tones, should be modest, submissive, and respectful; not loud, disrespectful. If at any time your opinion and theirs seem not to be in line, your views should be expressed, not with an act of dispute but with the meekness.

Your obedience to them should be uniform, you should not be obedient to the father and be disobedient to your mother. Parental obedience is generally rendered without much difficulty when the parents are present, but not always with the same ease when they are absent. Obedience should also be prompt, that is, it should be carried out as soon as the command is uttered. It is disrespectful of any child that it should be necessary for a father or a mother to repeat a command several times before it is done, that is reluctant obedience, which is not good enough. Also, the obedience should be cheerful, a grudging and murmuring obedience is quite disrespectful.

Submission to the family discipline and rule is no less your duty than obedience to commands

In every family there are rules that the children must abide by, as well as manners of discipline, reward, and punishment to these rules, and the children are expected to be subjected to these rules. Submission requires, that if at any time you have behaved in a way that calls for you to be punished by your parents, you should accept such punishments feeling sorry for doing it, and not be infuriated to anger, argument or disobedience to comply to the punishment. Your parents are an agent that makes sure you are on the right track, they wouldn't do anything to hurt you or make you feel any unnecessary pain.

You ought to make them proud of you

This is one of the best ways to repay your parents for all they have done for you. How do you make your parents proud of you? It is by performing well academically, facing your studies squarely, carrying out your house chores regularly, being a child of good reports at school, and other non-academic activities you find yourself doing. Anything that you won't be bold enough to tell your parents you did, don't do it! That's just the simple logic behind it.

What are My Parents' Obligations to Me?

Of course, your parents also have responsibilities towards you to ensure your confident living, which I'm sure they've been carrying out from the day you were born. The most important responsibility being that they must be able to provide your basic needs which are food, clothing and shelter. Likewise, parents also have the responsibility to provide necessary medical care for their children. If parents do not provide the children with life-saving medical treatment, the government may intervene against the parents' wishes. Additionally, your parents must also ensure that you satisfy school attendance requirements, in the same path, they can decide whether your education will be in a public school, a private school or through homeschooling, provided the reasons for such decisions are tangible and obvious.

Furthermore, your parents should teach you to gradually function Independently. This is because relying on your parents for everything and every decision might make you too dependent on them and probably restrict your free will as an individual in the long run. If you grow up relying on your parents for everything you have to do, this might affect your ability to make decisions independently as an adult. It is the parents' duty to teach their child age-appropriate skills in order to allow them to become more and more independent. A time will come when you will need to learn how to emotionally control yourself, tie his shoes, write his name, tolerate and cope when someone teases him. Over time, your parents will teach you so you develop more and more advanced skills. With time, you'll know how to type on paper, make choices of friends, select activities you do, drive a car, and fill out a job application. They just have to make it clear to you that your level of responsibility will grow throughout his life

Also, your parents are to make tough decisions that are really important for you, sometimes these decisions may annoy you and cause you to get angry with them, but that's totally normal it indicates that they are doing their job. What even makes it more annoying is the fact that they may not give you sufficient explanations for making these decisions, they might simply say " it's not the right call", but that's part of their job, making the best decisions for you based on their experience. They know the implications of these decisions in the long run, they know how it will turn out, they know you're making decisions based on present pleasure and not future consequences which is dangerous.

Then, your parents need to do their best to give you a good life, not a boring life or a life with no enjoyment. They have to create time to be with you, to hear out your challenges, to be with you through every situation, ensure your emotional, mental and physical well-being. They must also appreciate you, how you are, what you are and your talents, while trying to help you with your excesses and problems. These and many others should be your parents' obligations towards you.

How can I be happy?

We are all in pursuit of a happy life in this world, whatever situation you find yourself in this world, I want you to know that you are your happiness, you decide when you want to be happy and when you want to be sad. Happiness doesn't lie in any particular age, place, or item, your happiness is in you, it is left to you to bring it forth. There are numerous things you can do to make you happy, some are listed here.

Let go of grudges

This is actually easier said than done, but you don't have to do it for the other person who wronged you. Sometimes, offering forgiveness or dropping a grudge is more about self-care than compassion for others. Think deeply about your relationships with others. Are you harboring any unpleasant thoughts towards someone? If so, consider reaching out to them in an effort to settle things. This doesn't have to be a reconciliation, you may just need to end the relationship or that friendship and move on with your life. The most effective way to be happy is to break your association with things that take happiness away from you. If reaching out is a hard thing for you to do, try getting your feelings out in a letter. You don't even have to send it to them. Just getting your feelings out of your mind and into the world can be liberating.

Make friends, be more social and make more positive memories

We are social beings, you are a social being, which means you need the company of others, and having close friends can make us happier. Do you miss anyone, Reach out to them. Do you miss that ice-cream, save and buy it, do you miss going to amusement parks? Create time and go there! Just make those positive efforts that make you happy. The best time to make new friends is at your age, when you become an adult, making new friends might not be so easy because you have a lot you're occupied with. But it's not about how many friends you have. It's about having friends that add meaning to your life, even if it's just with one or two people. Try getting involved in a local volunteer group or taking a class. Both can help to connect you with like-minded people in your area. And odds are, they're looking for friends, too.

Your silent search of companions doesn't have to be limited to other humans. Pets can provide you with similar benefits, according to multiple studies. Do you like animals, but you're not allowed to have a pet? Consider joining a local animal shelter to make some new friends — both human and animal.

 Make positive memories, every part in our brains can be strengthened through practice. If our brains are really good at remembering negative things that happen, it can be useful to strengthen the regions of the brain responsible for remembering positive things.

Give yourself a confidence boost

If you're making efforts to increase your happiness and you're thinking you can't be successful at it? You wouldn't. That's why it's so important to build confidence, to prove to yourself that you can increase your happiness. The best way to achieve this is by starting with simple skills, like showing gratitude or prioritizing spending time doing fun things.

Be grateful

Simply being grateful can give your mood a big boost, among other benefits. For example, a recent two-part study found that practicing gratitude can have a significant impact on feelings of hope and happiness. Start each day by thinking of one thing you're grateful for. You can do this while you're brushing your teeth or just waiting for that snoozed alarm to go off. As you go about your day, try to check out for pleasant things in your life. They can be big things, such as knowing that someone loves you, someone that cares about your well-being, and so on. But these things can also be little things, such as a classmate who shared his biscuits with you, that neighbor who waved to you. With a bit of practice, you may even become more aware of all the positive things around you.

Explore what happiness means to you

We all define happiness in different ways. When you know what happiness means to you, you'll have an easier time finding it. So explore happiness, in this case, find out what it means, what it looks like, and what it feels like to you so that you can more easily create happiness and live a life filled with more purpose.

Acknowledge the unhappy moments

A positive attitude is generally a good thing, but bad things happen to everyone. It's just part of life. If you get some bad news, make a mistake, or just feel like you're in a funk, don't try to pretend you're happy. Acknowledge the feeling of unhappiness, then, shift your focus toward what made you feel this way and what it might take to recover. However, make efforts to solve it, take a long walk outside in the cold evening, Talking it over with someone, especially your parents, pray about it, do things you like, work more on your talents, let the moment pass and take care of yourself. Remember, no one's happy all the time.

How do I know it's Love?

Love is a feeling of affection that you can't even explain. You just feel it when you see the item or the person. It is a state of the mind, it is an increased type of normal affection. How do you know whether you're in love with someone or something? You can fall in love with an idea, an item, a person, etc.

The person, idea or item is on your mind almost all the time

When you're in love, that entity you've developed affection for is always in the back of your mind. You might have a sudden thought to call them or check the item because you haven't set your eyes on it, you haven't spoken to them in a few hours or you go into a store with the intention of buying something for yourself and then end up buying something for the person too. When you merely like something or someone, you can brush it off and think of other things as you go about your day, but when you're in love, this person is always on your mind, you are physically, mentally and emotionally imagining the person or thing theoretically almost all the time. It is said to be a calm and secure reality you will crave all the time.

You're happy and just a little bit nervous

When you're in love, you're genuinely a happier person when you come across that thing or person. It's like you're on a natural high. The thought of spending time with such a person or using such item really excites you. But being in love with a particular thing also makes you a bit nervous. You're anxious for what the future holds, whether such feelings will last long, whether the person will like you love in return, whether the item will keep on making you happy for a long time. You just know that you want you're the feeling to last. What makes love more exciting is the uncertainty of its outcome, you are not sure what tomorrow holds and how it will end.

You want to bring them around your family and friends or show it to them

When you're really into someone, be it a mere friend, a classmate, an item you purchased that you love, you would want to bring such things into all aspects of your life. You want to introduce them to your family and friends with the hope that they'll really like them or like such item too because it would hurt you if they didn't.

Epistemology

What is the Truth?

Truth can be defined as what's right, what's real and what's obvious. Truth is the property of being the same with fact or reality. In everyday language, truth is typically attached to things that aim to represent reality or otherwise are similar to it, such as the beliefs of people, propositions, and statements made by people. Truth is usually seen as the opposite of what is false. The concept of truth is discussed and argued in different contexts, including philosophy, art, theology, and science. Most human activities are based upon the concept of truth, its nature as a concept is assumed instead of being topic of discussion; these include most of the sciences, law, journalism, and even in our everyday life. Some philosophers view Truth as a basic concept that cannot be explained in any terms that are more easily understood than it has already been understood. Generally, truth is viewed as the likeness of language or thought to a mind-independent world.

There are different theories on truth, these theories have been brought into existence based on reasoning from different views, out of these, the three predominant theories of truth put forth by philosophers are:

Pragmatic theory of truth: According to this theory, anything that works is the truth. Let's take a look at these instances

From a counterintuitive view, that is, a view that opposes the natural way of thinking, for example, there are some true beliefs which are not very useful e.g., the belief that a cat has grey and white fur, and some false beliefs which may turn out to be very useful e.g., a blogger's false belief that people actually read their contents might be a useful motivation to encourage them to continue creating more contents.

Another instance under the pragmatic view of relativism that is checking the truth in one condition relative to another condition. Imagine two individuals who hold opposing beliefs about a particular concept. On the pragmatic view, as long as these contradictory beliefs are useful for the respective individuals who hold them, we would have to conclude they are both true. But in this situation, then truth is relative, a view which itself can not be defended.

Coherence theory of truth: This theory opines that truth is logical coherence, that is, a logical agreement of parts, among a set of beliefs an individual holds. Let's take a look at this instance under the coherence theory of truth. This instance is a view that supports that opposite statements can be true. On this view, it is possible for two different people to hold opposite beliefs, yet both beliefs might turn out to be "true" as long as these beliefs agree with each individual's idea of belief respectively. This leads to the ridiculous notion that opposite statements can both be true.

Finally, there is the correspondence theory of truth: this theory holds that truth is when an idea, belief, or statement matches with the way the world actually is, in other words, it matches with reality. This may rightly be called the "common sense" view of truth. In this sense, reality is the marker of truth, and the idea, belief, or statement is the truth-bearer. When the truth-bearer matches the truth-maker, they are said to stand in what is called "an appropriate correspondence relationship," which means the correct manner of similarity or correct manner of likeness, and truth is obtained. Consider these statements:

Donald Trump is the current President of the United States.

The city of Los Angeles is located in California

Dogs have four limbs

Trees have leaves

The sun is hot

New York is located in the United States of America.

Bats can fly

Are these statements true? They are true only if they match reality. Statement number 1 is true if, in reality, Donald Trump is the current President of the United States. Statement 7 is true if bats have been seen flying.

What is Knowledge?

Knowledge is knowing what to do, know how things are, or knowing a particular entity. It is the awareness, or understanding of someone or something, such as facts, information, descriptions, or skills, which is gotten through experience or education by experiencing, discovering, or learning. Knowledge can refer to the practical understanding of a subject. It can be implicit that is with practical skill or expertise or explicit which means it is with a clear understanding of a subject, it can be more or less formal. In philosophy, the study of knowledge is called epistemology. Plato popularly defined knowledge as "justified true belief", though this definition is now thought by some philosophers to be problematic because of the "Gettier problems" concept while others defend the platonic definition.

The process of getting knowledge involves complex important processes: perception, communication, and reasoning; while knowledge is also said to be related to the capacity of acknowledgment in human beings. Some processes of obtaining knowledge are:

Knowing by Acquaintance

When you know a person and you have a direct interaction with him or her. Otherwise, at most, you should claim only that it is almost as if you know him or her. You can have the knowledge about someone either from what you've been told about the person, from what you've read about the person or what the person does. Nonetheless, could you know facts about a person without ever meeting him or her? If so, there could well be a kind of knowledge which is different from knowing a fact; maybe knowing a thing or entity is distinct from knowing a fact about that thing or entity.

Knowledge-wh

There is a far wider range of ways in which we talk and think, using the term 'know'. Here are some of them collectively referred to as Knowledge-wh, knowledge where, knowledge who, knowledge- what, knowing-why, Knowing whether it is 4 p.m.; knowing who is due to visit; knowing why a visit is needed; knowing what the visit is meant to accomplish; knowing how that outcome is best achieved; and so forth.

Knowing-How

This kind is about knowing how it is that something is so; this is quite likely a form of knowledge-that. What is meant by 'knowing how' was one's knowing how to do something: knowing how to read the time on a clock, knowing how to call a friend, knowing how to cook a particular meal, and so forth. These seem to be skills or at least abilities.

What is the Difference between Knowledge and Belief?

In the previous headings, many definitions have been given to knowledge, however, in the search of truth and wisdom, Plato happened to be the first philosopher to define knowledge. In his writings, Plato described knowledge as true belief with an account. Although, starting with Plato's statement, other philosophers have usually defined knowledge as "true opinion combined with definition or sensible explanation". Plato went further to suggest that knowledge could be perception or sensation, just true belief, or true belief backed up by a rational account of itself. Therefore, we can assume that, there are three minimum conditions for knowledge,

-The entity must be true

-We must actually believe it.

Justification must be present which means, there must be sufficient evidence to back it up. Therefore, what is known has to be fact and thus true must come from the regard of the person acknowledging it as truth. The person must have an adequate basis for believing it. Regardless, it is generally adopted to be that 'traditional' theory of knowledge is "Justified true belief" this definition of knowledge contains the three attributes given to knowledge. This is just telling us that, we can have knowledge only of what is true.

However, the purpose of belief is to represent the world correctly. Therefore, belief serves its role only if the formation, remembering and revision of belief are sensitive to what one takes to be one's evidence. In the definition of belief, "Belief is an aspect of presentable attitude that is made known by their having the mind-to-world notion of it". Most philosophers have assumed that belief is an inner state of mind, directly accessible to self-analysis and distinct from, though casually related to, the believer's behavior. Thus, belief plays a central role in theoretical reasoning, which is the reason for what is so and therefore, has a role in practical, which is the reasoning about what to do. We, therefore, need to know what we can do and how we can do is related to what we want. When seeking knowledge of these things we seek true belief about them. By implication, what we do is based on what we believe.

Furthermore, knowledge is valuable, it is important to know the truth about our beliefs. It enables us to rely on our beliefs and the beliefs of others. Beliefs aim at the greater truth and are successful when they achieve it. Knowledge talks about the truth. The one who knows is the one who reaches the target of truth dependably. We, human beings are interested in knowledge because we are interested in the truth of our belief and the search for knowledge is the search for justification, which guarantees the truth. Knowledge, therefore, requires belief. Definitely, not all beliefs provide you with knowledge. Belief is necessary but not sufficient for knowledge. We are all sometimes mistaken in what we believe; in other words, while some of our beliefs are true, others are false. In simple terms, we can put it in this form, belief is something belief in, an opinion, it is the mental acceptance of a proposition or idea without the complete intellectual knowledge to verify its truth, while knowledge is a justified belief, it is a belief that has been backed up by sufficient evidence.

What is Skepticism?

Skepticism in one word means Doubt. Skepticism is the attitude of doubting and questioning knowledge claims or statements that are put forth in various areas. Skeptics have challenged the certainty or reliability of these statements by asking what principles they are based upon, any physical evidence to demonstrate it or what they actually establish. Skepticism involves questioning whether some claims or statements are truly the way they're said, and they are totally and necessarily true. Skepticism challenges the normal rational grounds of accepted assumptions. In everyday life, practically everyone is skeptical about some knowledge claims; but philosophical skeptics have doubted the possibility of any knowledge asides the knowledge that is obtained from directly felt experience, and can be experienced over and over again by others. This is simply telling us that "Seeing is Believing" or better still, "Experiencing is Believing".

Skepticism developed alongside various disciplines in which people claimed to have knowledge. Nearly everything was questioned, for example, whether one could obtain any certain knowledge; the philosophical study of the basic nature, structure, or elements of reality, or in the sciences. In ancient years, the most popular form of skepticism was medical skepticism, which, probably due to their limitations at that time, questioned whether one could know with a hundred percent assurance, either the causes, cures or prevention of diseases. Coming to ethics, doubts were raised about accepting various ideas and customs and about laying down any objective basis for making judgments of value. Skeptics of religion have questioned the doctrines of different religions, their acts, their way of life, their concepts.

Philosophical skepticism occurs in several forms. There's the radical forms of philosophical skepticism, this form of skepticism denies that knowledge or rational belief is possible and urge us to suspend judgment on many or all matters causing arguments. The other form of skepticism which has been viewed as a more moderate form holds that nothing can be known with certainty, or that we can know little or nothing about non-empirical matters, non-empirical matters are topics that are not backed up by evidence, they're more of theories rather than evidence. Even in our modern day to day lives, skepticism happens all around us, it's either the police officer who was skeptical that the driver, who was weaving in and out of traffic, only had two beers, or the teacher being skeptical when Timmy told her the dog ate his homework, or the common example of the politician said he would not raise taxes, and the voters were skeptical.

Logic

Could Time Travel be possible?

Wait a minute, you're probably thinking about that series movie, The Flash, where he runs and runs into the future, past and comes back to the present, that's just a movie with its own concept. Besides if you observe well enough, you'll notice some things do not add up as regards time travelling in that movie. Time travel is the concept of movement between certain points in time, similar to movement between different points in space by an object or a person, typically with the use of an imaginary device known as a time machine. Time travel is a popular concept in philosophy and fiction.

Since we are talking about time, we have to include the concept of presentism. Presentism is a philosophical concept that holds that the future and the past exist only as changes that will occur or have occurred to the present, and they have no real existence of their own. In this view, time travel is impossible because there is no future or past to travel to. Nevertheless, this has created a debate that even if past and future objects do not exist, there can still be definite truths about past and future events, and thus it is possible that a future truth about a time traveler deciding to travel back to the present date could explain the time traveler's actual appearance in the present

Another vital concept in the topic of time travelling is the Grandfather Paradox. The Grandfather Paradox appears to be the most important objection to the logical possibility of going back in time. This paradox has proven effective when it comes to convincing many people that travelling back in time is impossible. The concept that true time-travel is flatly impossible arises from the well-known "paradoxes" involved in it. A cogent example is "Perhaps you go back into the past and kill your grandfather when he was still a little boy, let's also assume in the present world they're still alive, what happens to the present form of your grandfather If you kill his past form? What happens to your parents that are alive? What happens to you? Who will give birth to your parents? Who will give birth to you? So we can see how these paradoxes are complex and hopeless and the easiest way to avoid this irrational chaos that results is to suppose that true time-travel is, and forever will be, impossible.

If everyone could travel into one's past and probably correct mistakes, what meaning does living make? What happens to people that have chosen to live a normal life without changing anything? What events do these changes set in motion? If one man could go back to 1914 and stop the first world war, what happens to the documents that already have the records of the war? This seems to give rise to all sorts of logical problems.

Could the Multiverse be Real?

Uni means one, in this concept, one world. Multi means many, in this context multiple worlds.

The concept of multiverse is the idea that our Universe, and all that is in it, including us, is just one small part of a larger structure. This larger entity covers our observable Universe as a minute part of a larger reality that extends beyond the limits of what we can see. That entire structure — which is the larger part of other universe that we can't observe — may itself be part of a larger entity that includes many other, disconnected Universes, which may or may not be similar to the Universe we live. If we are to focus on the eternal cosmic inflation theory which proposes that everything started with a Big Bang. It is suggested that as our Universe expanded into existence, it started off rapidly, then graduate in similar manner when you inflate a balloon.

This rapid bang did not only create our Universe but also gave rise to other universes in a vast bubble-like multiverse. While parts of the universe stopped the extremely rapid expansive increase and got separated to become normal space, nonetheless, large parts of the Universe have continued to inflate even now and those increasing portions keep producing new bubble universes. It will never stop as it is responsible for uncounted trillions of new universes budding off every second, according to the eternal cosmic inflation theory. Likewise, the theory is of the opinion that some of these bubbles in the multiverse are still hot and increasing rapidly, while others, like our own Universe, have slowed and cooled to enable the formation of stars, planets, galaxies, etc.

This concept may seem a little confusing, but it becomes even more complex when you actually start thinking about its consequences. If the multiverse theory is correct, then there's a universe out there where everything is exactly like this universe, you may exist but you'll have a different life entirely or doing different things at a particular time. Again, you're thinking of the same series movie, The Flash, in the movie, the earth we live in is regarded as earth 1, there's earth 2,3 till earth who knows? According to the storyline, an event occurred that linked all these Earths to one another such that with a particular device, a person in earth 1 can travel to earth 2 or any earth, or from any earth to another earth at all. Barry who is the speedster in earth 1, turns out to be a policeman in earth 2. Our observable universe goes only as far as light has traveled in our universe's existence, which is about 13.7 billion light-years. The space-time beyond the boundary of our universe would essentially be considered as its own universe. Some debate that there has to be something beyond our universe and possibly, it might be another universe.

Why Do People Dream?

I'm sure at one point or the other, you've experienced something similar to watching a movie with your eyes closed while sleeping. It's more like watching yourself do something, that's a dream. Dreams are basically visual activities and pictures that our mind creates while we sleep. They can look so real. Dreams can make you feel happy, sad, scared or not bothered at all depending on what you see related to what's happening to you in reality. And they may appear to be confusing or perfectly ordered. Dreams can happen at any time during sleep, but it is stated that we have our most vivid dreams during a phase called REM which stands for Rapid Eye Movement sleep when our brain is most active.

Some experts hold that we dream about three to four times in a night, however it has been hard for researchers to explain the role of dreams. When you're awake, your thoughts have a certain link to the dreams you have. When you sleep, your brain is still very much active, but your thoughts or dreams often make little or no sense. This may be due to the fact that emotional centers of the brain cause us to dream, rather than the logical regions of the brain. Though there's no physical proof, dreams are usually bothering thoughts based on your recent activities, conversations, or other issues in your life. However, there are some popular theories that define the roles of dreams:

Dreams as your source of inspiration: One theory that promotes the reason we dream is that it helps to bring out our creative tendencies. Artists of all kinds give appreciations to their dreams for inspiring them to carry out some of their most creative work. You may have woken up times in your life with a great idea for a movie or a song just because of a word or scenario you saw in your dream. Also, dreams serve as memory assistants since dreams are basically stories and images that our mind develops while we sleep. There is a high chance that what you dream about might be things that happened in the past or that moment when you were being taught a particular topic in school.

One commonly held theory about the purpose of dreams is that they help you keep important memories and things you've learned, get rid of unimportant memories, show you things to happen and help you with difficult thoughts and feelings. If you learn new information and sleep on it, you'll be able to remember it better than if asked to remember that information without the benefit of sleep. How dreams influence memory storage isn't understood yet. But dreams may help the brain more efficiently store important information while blocking out occurrences that could slow down with memory and learning

One of the most significant influences on dreams is how much or how little you're sleeping. Being sleep-deprived for a night or more can cause parts of your brain to be more active when you enter into REM (Rapid Eye Movement) sleep. You're likely to have more dreams that look so real if you've had some restless nights. You're also more likely to recall those dreams. Increased hormone production increases the way your brain processes thoughts and emotions. This often causes some intense dreams.

Furthermore, mental health issues such as depression and anxiety, and other mood-related conditions, can cause intense and sometimes disturbing or negative dreams and nightmares. The medications for these conditions, including antidepressants and antipsychotics, are also associated with a higher risk of nightmares. The notion is that if you go to bed with a disturbed mind, you may wake with a solution or at least feel better about the situation. Some dreams may help our brains process our thoughts and what happened during the day. Other dreams may just be the result of normal brain activity and may be insignificant.

If Someone makes a clone of you, are you still you?

The term cloning refers to a number of different processes that can be used to produce genetically identical copies of a biological entity. The copied material, which has the same genetic units as the original, is called a clone. Therefore, if a clone of you is created it looks similar to you physically, however, there are certain things that differ the original and replica.

Firstly, the womb where your clone will develop will not be your mother's womb or the same womb you developed. This already creates a significant difference. Even if a clone was developed in your mother's womb, she will now be older, her body conditions have changed and no two pregnancies are alike. In line with this, the parents that raise your clone will be different; even if you plead with your parents that are now aging to adopt your clone, your parents are now different. They may also act differently towards the clone, provide him with a different version of parenthood entirely. They would expect certain behaviors or things from your clone or try to prevent things that "went wrong" while they were bringing you up. Nevertheless, your clone will grow up in a different world, with different environmental challenges and also, with different technology influencing his mode or thinking. The clone will go through a different school system, different entertainment styles and trends too.

Furthermore, your clone will obtain different experiences from yours. He may have a really bad math teacher, and end up disliking and being afraid of math instead of making math his best subject like you. He may grow up to love dogs, unlike you who is scared of dogs because a big German Shepherd bit you when you were little. All these show that your clone may look like you, but it is not you! Your clone will not be you although, he may have similar personality features, but his mind will not be exactly like your mind. He may react similarly to you in some situations, while in others, very differently. And that's probably the reason companies that specialize in cloning dogs and cats, will guarantee the clone will look like very close to your dead beloved pet, but they will not give you a hundred percent assurance that it will have the same quality.

Aesthetics

What is Beauty?

The term "beauty" is basically associated with aesthetic experience and typically refers to an essential quality of a particular item that stirs up some type of reaction in the human observer, the reaction could be pleasure, calm, anxiety, admiration, or delight. Beauty is linked to both natural things around us such as sunsets or mountains, as well as to human-made art works such as paintings. There have been several theories over the years of Western philosophical thought that attempt to define "beauty," by either:

Linking it to "important qualities" within the natural creation or the man-made work of art, or regarding it entirely in terms of the experience of beauty by the human subject. The former statement considers beauty as being objective, this means that it refers to beauty as something that exists in its own right, internally, in the "something" or art object, and can be experienced independently. Meanwhile, the other strategy regards beauty to be subjective, in other words, it sees beauty as something that occurs in the mind of the subject who perceives beauty, more like beauty lies in the eyes of the beholder. In Aesthetics, the topic of objectivity versus subjectivity has been a matter of serious philosophical debate not only with regard to the nature of beauty but it also comes up in matters relating to judging the relative advantages of pieces of art, as we will notice this in topics relating to aesthetic judgement. But basically, what we're trying to find out is whether beauty itself exists in the object, that is the natural phenomenon or the artifact, or purely within the subjective experience of the object.

Let us consider the objectivist views of beauty by citing some instances, according to Plato, beauty exists in its field of the Forms. Beauty is objective, it is not about the experience of the observer. Plato's conception of objectivity is different from the usual concepts. The world of Forms is immaterial rather than material, in other words, for Plato, forms, and beauty, are non-physical ideas. Yet beauty is objective in that it is not a feature of the observer's experience.

Likewise, Aristotle too promoted the concept of an objective view of beauty, but it had one major difference from Plato's objectivity concept. Aristotle stated that beauty resides in what is being observed and is defined by characteristics of the art object, such as symmetry, order, balance, and proportion, and this criterion is applicable to both natural and man-made objects. Even though they hold different conceptions of what "beauty" is, Plato and Aristotle do agree that it is a feature of the "object," and not something in the mind of who is observing it.

Coming to the Subjective point of View, some instances include David Hume, who argued that beauty does not lie in "things" but is entirely subjective, that is to say, it's a matter of feelings and emotion. Beauty is in the mind of the person who is looking at the object, and what is beautiful to one observer may not be beautiful to another. Furthermore, Immanuel Kant believed that aesthetic judgement depends on feelings, specifically, the feeling of pleasure. What gives a person pleasure is a matter of personal taste. Such judgements involve neither cognition nor logic, and are therefore subjective. Beauty is defined by judgement processes of the mind, it is not a feature of the thing judged to be beautiful.

A complex situation arises with a purely subjective account of beauty because the idea of beauty becomes meaningless if everything is merely a matter of taste or personal preference. If beauty is purely in the eye of the beholder, the idea of beauty has no value as an ideal comparable to truth or goodness. Arguments arise over matters of taste; people can have strong opinions regarding whether or not beauty is present, suggesting that perhaps there are some standards. However, some are of the strong opinion that beauty exists deep in our minds. It's a gift handed down from the intelligent skills and rich emotional lives of our most ancient ancestors. The way we react to images, to the expression of emotion in art, to the beauty of music, to the night sky, will be with us and our descendants for as long as the human race exists.

Could One thing be Beautiful and ugly at the same time?

You might have come across a painting or a mosaic, a mosaic is simply a painting with papers. At a first look, or from afar, the overall work seems pleasing, attractive and pleasurable, but as you move closer and observe what is actually being painted in the art work, and you find out that the picture being painted itself isn't so attractive in real sense. Yes, the entire work looks beautiful and attractive, but a deeper look shows a rather ugly image. What do we call this, aesthetically ugly? Could one thing be beautiful and ugly at the same time? Yes. However, this majorly depends on the preferences of the observer, the experience and notion about what is actually being painted. Different people have different views about different things, that's simply the idea behind it. In the same way you take certain pictures and you really like them, and you show it to your friend, and he's like "Common, who's that? Delete it". Since it has been stated that there's no physical standard for measuring beauty, only way to separate what's beautiful from things we see as being ugly is through what we prefer individually, and by relating it to another thing.

What is Art?

Art is a very wide range of human activities that include creating visual, auditory, or performed works of art that express the author's imaginative or technical skill, and are aimed to be appreciated for their beauty or emotional power. The oldest documented forms of art are visual arts, which include images or objects in fields like painting, sculpture, printmaking, photography, and other visual media. Architecture is also mentioned as one of the visual arts; however, like the decorative arts, it involves the developing objects where the practical considerations of use are important, in a way that they usually are not in another visual art, like a painting.

Art may be grouped in terms of its representation of reality, expression, communication of emotion, or other qualities. Though the definition of what makes up art is being discussed and has changed over time, general descriptions center on the idea of imaginative or creative skill coming from human ideas and creation. When it comes to visually identifying a work of art, there is no single set of values or aesthetic traits, this is simply telling us that a baroque painting will not necessarily share many features with a contemporary performance piece, but they are both considered art.

A fundamental purpose common to most art forms is the basic intention to appeal to, and connect with, human emotion. However, the term is very broad and is divided into several sub-categories that lead to satisfactory, decorative, therapeutic, communicative, and intellectual ends. As a matter of fact, art may be considered an expression of the human condition, or a product of the human experience. The decorative aspect of arts add aesthetic and design values to our homes, environment, and even everyday objects, such as a glass or a chair, changing them from a mere household object to something that is aesthetically beautiful.

The meaning of art is influenced by the intentions of the artist as well as the feelings and ideas it causes in the viewer. The meaning of art is often specific in terms of different cultures, it is shared among the members of a given society and dependent upon cultural context. The purpose of works of art may be to communicate political, spiritual or philosophical ideas, to create a sense of beauty, to explore the nature of perception, for pleasure, or to generate strong emotions. In fact, its purpose may be non-existent. Art, in a general sense, is a form of communication. It means whatever the artist intends it to mean, and this meaning is shaped by the materials, techniques, and forms it makes use of, as well as the ideas and feelings it creates in its viewers. Art is a channel of expressing feelings, thoughts, observations, things happening around, things to happen, and so on.

Moreover, sometimes beauty is not the artist's ultimate goal. Art is often intended to look appealing to, and connect with, human mind and emotion. Artists may express something so that their audience is moved in some way, either by means of creating feelings, religious faith, curiosity, interest, identification with a group, memories, thoughts, or creativity. For instance, performance art often does not always aim to please the audience but instead bring certain feeling upon them, reactions, conversations, or questions from the viewers.

Axiology

What has Value?

In the real sense, we'll say anything that is good to us, anyone that is important to us, anything that helps us, anyone that helps us, anything that's a priority on our mind at a point in time, our role models, our mentors, our parents, relatives, anything that we so much like. All these have values to us. But generally, anything that improves the situations of the society, anything that has virtue and promotes the good of the society, all these have attached values.

Values are basic beliefs that guide or motivate our behaviors or actions. Our values help us to determine what is important to us. Values describe the personal qualities we choose to copy in order to guide our actions; the kind of person we want to be; the way we treat ourselves and others, and our interaction with the world around us. In other words, values provide the general guidelines for conduct. Values in a narrow sense is that which is good, desirable, or worthy. Values are the motive behind purposeful decisions and actions, they are the ends to which we act and come in many forms. Personal values are personal beliefs about right and wrong and may or may not be considered moral. Cultural values are values accepted by religions or societies and reflect what is important in each of these aspects. Talking about traditions, the custom, way of life, way of doing things, are the entities that have value. Religious wise, the valuable entities are the beliefs, concepts, doctrines, lifestyle etc.

Value specifies a relationship between a person and a goal, this implies that anything that helps you to achieve your goals at that point in time, has a value. However, valuable entities are relational in the sense that what one person values may not be what another person values even in the same situation. For example, a person who values honesty might blow the whistle on financial wrongdoing by a superior whereas another person who values loyalty may remain silent. This is an example of values conflict. The honest person may believe there are limits to loyalty and keeping quiet about a wrongful act out of loyalty might harm others. The loyal person may believe in the importance of keeping one's confidence even if it might harm others because of the trusting relationship.

Some value entities stand the test of time; they are always good or rightful behavior. For example, virtues such as honesty and kindness. It is difficult to imagine having a good friendship with people without them because these virtues help to build trust in relationships. There are always exceptions, but they are very few. For example, if a criminal who intends to do harm to your friend knocks on the door and asks whether you have seen the friend, you're probably not going to say yes and you shun out of a sense of honesty. Here, the greater good, so to speak, is to protect your friend from harm. Furthermore, values can either be intrinsic or extrinsic value. Intrinsic value is something that has value in its own right, such as honesty and kindness, whereas extrinsic value is doing something for another reason such as to get wealth and fame.

Is Money Really Valuable

On a particular afternoon, a group of young people who had just recently graduated decided to visit their favorite lecturer at his house. These graduates had been out of school for almost a year and they were each talking about their experiences and complaining about the outside world, life after school and dealing with all of the frustrations and confusion that come with it. They complained about the long hours, the demanding bosses, the competitive job market, and how all anybody seemed to talk about or care about was the money! After a while, the professor got up and made some tea. He got out six cups, one for each of his former students. Three of these cups happened to be cheap disposable cups and the other three were made of his nice ceramics. He then invited everyone to get up and pick for themselves.

Within seconds the arguments had already begun. "Wait, why do you get that cup?" "No, let me have it, I drove here." "No way, I got here first, go get your own." They all laughed and gently pure behind the issue about who got to drink what out of what. A silent competition among friends. When they were done and finally sat back down the lecturer smiled and said, "You see? This is your problem. You are all arguing over who gets to drink out of the nice cups when all you really wanted was the coffee."

Money is a touchy subject. That's because most of us, to a certain extent, associate a lot of our self-worth and identity to our job and how much money we make. Money can be said to be a market valuation of our skills and competence as a person, and therefore we all get a little bit testy and move around uncomfortably in our chairs whenever issues related to money is brought up.

But money is merely a reasonable store of value, it is not value itself. There are many stores of value in life. Time and knowledge are forms of value. Likewise, happiness and other positive emotions are forms of value. Money is often just a means of exchanging these various forms of value with one another. Money is not the cause of wealth in one's life, the cause of wealth is the effect of money on one's life. Money is fluid. Its value only becomes actualized when it's put into use, that being said, we can draw that money is a reflection of the owner's values and intentions. Money is totally neutral. It's merely a vessel for the exchange of experience between two people. You make your money by creating experiences for others, you then give your money to others to receive experiences in return. For instance, when you buy some material good like a nice dress, you're not just buying the physical goods, you're also buying the experience of wearing that necklace, you're buying the experience of social status that's associated with it. You're buying that ornament to your identity, that knowledge of what owning and using it feels like and whether it makes you happy or not.

However, judging by the world we are, money seems to be a valuable entity, if not the most valuable, pretty probably because most of the things we intend to achieve, our aims are all related to one word, Money! An adult secures a job, wakes up early to go to work, just to make money to be able to feed you, cater for you and pay for your school fees. You on the other hand, as you grow up, you go to school, from college to the university, to being a graduate, to probably Post graduate studies, then securing a job, by now you're an adult. You wake up early to go to work and work for several hours a day so you can cater for your children and pay their school fees, you see the cycle now?

Money is valuable, but it isn't a form of value.

Political Philosophy

What is Freedom?

What is Freedom?

Freedom is generally understood as independence of the conscious; will of an individual, as opposed to slavery. A slave is constantly subjected to the will of another person, item, act etc. A free person can do whatever he chooses as long as he does not break the law and affect the freedom of others. If your freedom affects the freedom of other people, then it is described as "negative liberty, because it assumes you're trying to make a point that the freedom of such people ends where yours begin, which is not supposed to be so.

Freedom also includes a sense of inner freedom which exists where free will is backed up by free action. A person who keeps on failing at a particular aim he/she wants to achieve is in a sense, unfree, he's a slave to that particular situation at that time frame. His will is not free because it is subject to thoughts relating to what's holding him back from accomplishing what he had determined to do, for instance, a person who is an addict. He may want to give up his addiction but cannot and the decisions he makes are influenced by the need to satisfy the addiction. So, we can that in some situations, freedom comes from self-control. Goethe said, "From the forces that all creatures bind, who overcomes himself his freedom finds."

Complete freedom includes the inner freedom of the will and the external freedom of the environment such that a person's plans are not restricted by either himself or some other agency. Freedom is not a value but is the basis of values because it allows a person to create and appreciate values, to pursue the classical values of beauty, truth, honesty, contentment, self-reliance, and so on. It enables people to use their creativity so as to bring joy to God and to others, their family, relatives, friends and wider community

Freedom is also attached to the idea of responsibility. George Bernard Shaw stated that "Liberty means responsibility. That is why most men dread it." A free person has the opportunity and burden of making choices and decisions. This also means that he must bear the consequences of his actions. Freedom allows people to pursue their interests within the permission of law. It means that people are not controlled and not part of someone else's plans and purposes. Moreover, as long as they do not break the law which is a system of general rules that apply to everyone, they can live where they choose, follow whatever career they wish, trade without restriction, read and write what they like, accept whatever beliefs and opinions they hold, associate with whomever they wish and form clubs, groups, parties and sects without asking anyone's permission. In short, they have the freedom to follow their conscience, and such a person would naturally live within the moral law. And in case the person does things that are against the law or affects the freedom of others, there will be punishments which might include taking away such person's external freedom.

What is the difference between Justice and Revenge?

The terms revenge and justice are often confused with each other, and that's somehow expected to happen. This has been the case right from the old ages, however, as meanings changed and evolved over time, the concept of these two words have increasingly become more different, therefore they're not used to refer to the same things anymore. To begin with, it would be right to state that justice is fair and revenge is not. Mostly, revenge is carried out depending on underlying conditions, motivations, or intentions, these might be either just or unjust, fair or much more brutal compared to the wrong that was originally done. Judging from that, we can say that revenge is mainly emotional, while justice is rational.

Revenge is mostly about "acting out" through acts of violence and negative emotions. If it is nurtured and done every time, the avenger may think there's actual pleasure experienced in causing others to suffer for the hurt they've caused him/her. Justice is logical, legal, and ethical. Justice is defined isn't really about getting even or experiencing a sort of satisfaction in retaliation. Instead, it's about righting a wrong that most members of society as opposed to simply the alleged victim, would agree is morally wrong. Justice is not emotional and in real sense, this makes it unbiased. The morality of justice is based on cultural or community standards of fairness and equity. Whereas revenge has a certain self-centered quality attached to it, justice is selfless in that it relies on non-self-interest, established law.

Furthermore, revenge is, by nature, personal; while justice is impersonal, impartial, and it is a social and legal phenomenon. The driving force behind revenge is to get even, to carry out a private motive, or to achieve what might be referred to as personal justice. On the other hand, justice is impersonal. It is majorly about moral correction in situations where certain ethical and culturally vital principles have been violated. When justice is successfully meted out, the outcome benefits or protects both the individual and society which can operate effectively only when certain acceptable behavioral guidelines are followed.

Moreover, revenge is about retaliation, justice is about restoring balance. The aim of revenge has mostly to do with expressing anger or hatred. It's a form of payback, and its major intent is to harm. Revenge is not primarily about justice but about victims' expressing their inborn tendency to retaliate against any wrong done to them. Meanwhile, justice is concerned with bringing back balance through equality. It centers on fairness. Justice seeks to be as even as possible. Justice is not entirely about doing the other side "one better" but about properly punishing wrongdoing.

What would happen if the Law is the same for all?

What is the law? The law is the guiding principle that directs and instructs us about what we're expected to do, how to do things and things that we shouldn't do. And if in any case, the law is broken by anyone, there will be punishments. There's something called the Rule of law, this means that the law rules over everyone and anyone, and generally, we are all equal before the law. The law that applies to the oldest citizen also applies to the youngest citizen, there's no exception. The statement that we are all equal before the law is something that has helped our society significantly.

If the law is the same for all, everyone will have equal chances of achieving things, there will be law and order, everyone would do what they're expected to do out of a free mind and most importantly, there won't be misuse of power by those in government. Additionally, it will promote virtues such as integrity, the right attitude to work, contentment, and put an end to abusing other people's rights.

Conclusion

What are the values of philosophy? Uncountable! It's natural to wonder, to think, to ask questions, to find out, and discover why things are the way they are. It doesn't make you strange, it's perfectly normal. At your age, this is the best time to work towards becoming wonderful philosophers, your names might even enter the books of philosophy one day, who knows? Keep on observing, keep on asking, keep on thinking, keep on knowing and keep on achieving, enjoy nature!

Finally, if you enjoyed this book, please let me know your thoughts with a short review on Amazon. All that you need to do is to click the blue link next to the yellow stars that says "customer reviews." You'll then see a gray button that says "Write a customer review"—click that and you're good to go. It means a lot, thank you!

Loria